Brave
Wise
Woman

Brave
Wise
Woman

TRANSFORM THE FALLOUT OF YOUR
BREAKUP INTO YOUR POWER

JEN LEGASPI

For more information, email jen@jenlegaspi.com.

ISBN: 979-8-88759-125-4

A Gift from Me to You

I've created a companion resource to support your journey towards meeting your
Brave Wise Woman.

8 Powerful Intentions to Awaken Your Brave Wise Woman

To receive your gift,
visit www.bravewisewoman.com
(or scan the QR code).

You will also join a community of women who will receive exclusive tips and offers for upcoming programs to help you meet your
Brave Wise Woman.

Dedication

For all the smart "good girls" who believe they have to be perfect to fly.

Author's Note

I wrote parts of this book based on my memories, personal experiences, and perceptions of people and events to illustrate how I believe they influenced my life. I am grateful to have learned from them. Some memories might be less than perfect, especially those from my childhood, but I shared them to the best of my knowledge while staying close to my truth. It's helpful to note that people can experience the same event but have differing memories, opinions, and perspectives. Some events have been compressed. Any dialogue comes from my recollections and may not be a word-for-word account, but was written to reflect the essence of the conversation as I remember it. Names have been eliminated or changed to protect the anonymity of others involved.

Table of Contents

Introduction

the healer
you have been
looking for
is your own courage
to know and love
yourself completely

- yung pueblo, inward

S ignificant breakups can bring up a lot of fear. Fear of being alone, the future, or how we might navigate the pain. Many of us have go-to coping strategies—some conscious, others unconscious. My pattern throughout my life was to bounce from one relationship to another as quickly as possible. But I learned bravery emerges in how we choose to heal and start again.

It took a defining moment in my life—the end of my marriage—to ask the questions, *Who am I? Do I love myself?* I began searching for the answers within instead of through the lens of a relationship. I discovered I was the one who had been breaking my heart for decades and it was time to stop. My quest eventually awakened the Brave Wise Woman within me.

A Brave Wise Woman is who *we already are* but haven't met yet. She is the part of us that dwells in our truth and is (what I consider) an expression of our true or authentic self. When we meet her, we stop abandoning ourselves for the sake of love. We honor our needs and advocate for them without apology, shame, or fear. We find our power. Our relationships become more authentic because our words and actions align and we speak our truth. When we meet our Brave Wise Woman, self-love is the outcome.

My healing path to meet her was intuitively guided by curiosity and inquiry. And you can awaken her within you too.

What This Book Is and What You'll Learn

This is not a traditional memoir or a step-by-step self-help book. The content speaks to the universal experience of navigating the sudden ending of a relationship, its fallout, and the resulting search for truth, meaning, and healing. Through my stories, I share why the fallout of my breakup sparked my inner quest to know myself. I share how I dug up my beliefs and exposed my relationship patterns and their origins to start making positive changes in my life. Each lesson reveals what it took to navigate difficulty, heal, and start the journey towards meeting my most authentic version of self. At the end of each chapter, I invite you to try out the practices that paved my path toward meeting my Brave Wise Woman.

You will resonate with this book if you are:

- Experiencing a significant breakup or separation and divorce

- Wanting to take responsibility for making positive changes

- Curious about forging a deeper connection with yourself

- Seeking inspiration to heal and transform your life (and to know you aren't alone)

- Wanting to trust yourself more than you currently do

- Sensing your choices in romantic partners could be off

- Questioning if you are brave enough to stop breaking your own heart (Hint: You are!)

I'm a life coach, yoga teacher, friend, and sister on the path. I know what it's like to be smart but make questionable choices. I know how it feels to run unconscious patterns that give away my power. But I also know first-hand what it's like to discover my truth and make changes rooted in self-love. My relationship with myself has improved, as have my other relationships. I'm not a licensed therapist or psychologist. The contents of this book are not a substitute for the support of a licensed professional, especially for those experiencing abuse or trauma. These are stories and knowledge shared through the lens of my personal experience.

What I bring to the self-love dialogue is an example of how our innate curiosity can be a transformative teacher. We all have our answers inside of us. We are not broken or separate from the truth because the truth lives within, not outside of us. Discovering it starts the journey of empowering ourselves to make different choices in alignment with who we really are and co-creating the life we desire.

In the first chapter, I share how my defining moment in life helped me see I was the one breaking my own heart.

I hope this book inspires you to want to meet your Brave Wise Woman.

I

My Defining Moment

How My Breakup Helped Me See I was the One Breaking My Heart

On the day I graduated from my yoga teacher certification program, I received a text message from my husband notifying me he found an apartment and was moving out.

I was celebrating a rite of passage in the yoga world, one of stepping into the role of a teacher. It had taken me seventeen years as a diligent yoga student to arrive there. The day was an important one for my spiritual journey and yet, it was entangled in sorrow. I was still reeling from the "It's time we separate" bomb he dropped on me.

I had a strong sense that this moment marked an ending and a beginning, and I knew with all of my being that receiving *this text message* on *this specific day* could not be an accident. It was clear the Universe had another plan in mind for my life, one that would change me, though I did not know how. For the first time in my life, I had an instantaneous trust in something greater than myself.

I was a mess from how quickly it seemed my marriage ended. Major life events can do that: tear us apart, shake our core, and force us to question almost everything. Their transformative nature makes them a defining moment that can change who we are and what happens next in our life. The conditions become ripe for the new to emerge while something else inevitably falls away, including people, perceptions, and our identity. The end of my twelve-year relationship was my defining moment. What I did not know yet was the path I was about to take would eventually lead me to meet the Brave Wise Woman within.

Because I had not yet met my Brave Wise Woman—who I believe is an expression of my authentic self—I didn't even know I should want to. After all, I *thought I was already that person*. I had been on a spiritual path because of yoga and had done some inner work. But until I took a hard look at where I was not taking responsibility for my life, I could not discover her, unlock her power, and bring her into the light. She is ever present but was buried underneath my beliefs, unhelpful patterns, and view of the world. I had not yet taken responsibility because I didn't think I had a reason to.

I was comfortable within the container of marriage and being married to someone I believed was my person. When I met Brian, I noticed how well we got along from the start. He was smart and personable, and conversations between us seemed to flow. I even had a strong sense early on that I deserved to be with someone like him.

My friends and family liked him. Many had commented that they had never seen me so happy. And I was. I truly felt lucky. We made each other laugh and developed a strong friendship. I really trusted him.

Five years into our relationship, we got engaged. It was a sweet moment, one of the happiest in my life at that point. Close friends and family attended our wedding. We wrote our vows too, declaring our love and appreciation for each other and committing to honoring the truth between us. Early on, we used to say to each other we would never divorce, and we were always together after that, enjoying life and our time with each other and our dogs.

So, the night that marked the beginning of the end, I came apart at the seams.

***

As I was driving home from breakfast with my father one Saturday, Brian called to tell me he had to go to his office for a few hours to work on a presentation. He was leaving the next day for a business trip. Later that night, we had plans to go to a dinner party. A friend of ours had planned to pick us up and drive us there.

Since he was busy, I met up with a girlfriend for a glass of wine mid-afternoon. I invited him to join us after he was done but he was still at work. So, I finished up and went home to get dressed for the dinner party.

When our friend arrived to pick us up, he was still not home. I texted him again, but no response. This seemed odd to me, but I figured he was still preparing for his trip. As I left the house, I sent another message:

See you at the dinner party.

He never showed.

By 10:00 pm, my girlfriend and I thought it was strange that I hadn't heard from him, but I assumed he had worked late and went straight home instead. But when we entered the house, he wasn't there.

My heart jumped out of my chest. Panicking, I checked my phone for any new texts or missed calls, but I had none. Worst-case scenario thinking set in. Did he get in a car accident? Is he in the hospital? Dead? Convinced something bad had happened to him, I called another close friend for advice. He suggested I go to his workplace and look for his car in the parking lot.

Though I was panicking, I insisted on driving and was grateful my girlfriend wanted to come along with me. When we arrived at his office, the parking lot was empty. My heart was now pounding out of my chest.

We cruised by the local shops and bars to look for his car on the street, but when that proved fruitless, I drove home in tears, sick to my stomach.

I sent another text: *Where are you? I'm worried.*

No response.

My girlfriend kept me company a little longer, then went home. I waited for him, but by midnight, I was still alone. Soon after, he sent a text to signal he was OK. I tried to call him, but he didn't answer the phone, so I lay down in the guest room and tried to sleep.

When I got out of bed in the morning, I peeked into the other bedroom. He was there, asleep.

***

I wanted to wake him up and demand answers, but I didn't. I let him sleep in. *He probably needs the rest before his business trip.* I waited until after I came home from a yoga class that morning to ask what had happened.

"Where did you go last night?"

He explained he went out to listen to music and hung out with a few people he met at the venue.

"I would have joined you after the dinner party, had I known…"

Because he wanted to go alone, a part of me sensed something had shifted within him. But instead of paying attention to that, my instinct was to make it easy for him in the future.

"You know, if there's something you want to do by yourself, and we have other plans, all you have to do is say so. I was worried that something had happened to you."

He apologized.

My words that day did not match those of a worried, angry wife who was used to steady communication with her husband. I was afraid to ask more questions. I didn't realize that my fear of speaking up for myself at that moment was co-creating conditions for this situation to repeat.

It wasn't long before his taxi arrived to take him to the airport, and after the door shut behind him, I fell apart. Something felt off between us. Every night for the rest of the week, I was anxious and in tears. While he was gone, our communication was minimal. I became hypervigilant, obsessing about our relationship, and pulling every inch apart to see if I could uncover hints of what had just happened.

That emotional, anxiety-filled, obsessive week led me to an insight that was the first of what would be many to come. It planted the initial seed for my healing.

I recalled a time in our life when we were living together, and I had just been laid off from my job. I was unsure about my next career step, so while I was collecting unemployment, I took on side projects to help my friends with their small businesses. The work was not consistent and definitely not a full-time job.

While Brian was at work, I took care of the home—cleaned, shopped for groceries, ran miscellaneous errands, cared for our dogs, and cooked for us. It gave me a sense of purpose. I believed my contributions were of value then because *this is what one does if you aren't working*. Logistically, it made sense back then. It's just what I did.

And at first, he seemed to appreciate it, which I unconsciously translated as approval. So, for a while, I continued down the path of *not knowing* while also avoiding doing the work *to know* what I wanted to do next in my life.

Looking back, though, a part of me picked up on a part of him that may not have been as OK with it as I believed. It only takes a comment spoken under the breath to catch a whiff. But I wasn't in a place to address it yet, so I pretended not to notice. As I recalled that time in our life together, I became curious about why I couldn't face my situation head-on.

In exploring that, the answer emerged when I examined the model of marriage my parents had shown me. Until this moment, I had not considered my beliefs or their origins, but when I noticed the linkage, I realized I had unconsciously recreated my parents' model of marriage. My father was the breadwinner, and though my mother was active in our community, she primarily stayed home to raise me and my two siblings until my parents divorced. She wanted to go back to work sooner than the divorce, but my father didn't approve of that for our family. His belief seemed to be that *women stayed at home to raise the children*. And I ended up adopting the belief that *women/wives should not want more*. Our beliefs drive everything. They underpin our behavior, actions, and outcomes in life.

When I made this connection, I sensed that this was just the tip of the iceberg. I decided it might be time for me to explore therapy, not just because it might be good for me but because an unconscious part of me believed *I was at fault* for the current state of our relationship. I planned to share this with him when he returned from his trip.

Except I didn't have the opportunity to do so.

***

His flight was scheduled to arrive at about 5:30 pm. I sped home from my yoga teaching program, anxious about his return. It had been an emotionally exhausting week, and I was eager to discuss whatever was going on for him and share what I learned about myself. I had just enough time to feed the dogs and get settled before he'd walk in the door.

But as I approached our building, I noticed his car wasn't where it had been all week. Something wasn't right. *Did someone steal his car?*

I went into the kitchen to look for his car keys, where they had been all week. They weren't there. Denial dug in. *Did he ask someone to come into the house to pick up the keys and drive off with the car?*

I went into our bedroom and found a pile of dirty clothes in the closet. I had just done the laundry two days prior. As if that wasn't enough evidence, I went into the bathroom and touched the towel hanging off the shower door. It was wet.

After an anguishing week apart, realizing that he had taken an earlier flight home, showered, unpacked, and left the house before I returned home devastated me.

My calls to him rolled to voicemail, so I sent a text:

Where are you? I know you took an earlier flight.

An hour later, he replied to tell me he went out to eat. He didn't share where he was but I wanted to see him. I wrote back and asked if I could join him out for a drink.

No response.

Once again, I spent the rest of the night crying on the couch. I waited up for him as late as I could, then slept in the guest bedroom. In the morning, he was home, asleep in the other bedroom.

It should have been crystal clear something was amiss. Though he wanted to be alone, a part of me sensed he might be avoiding me. Still, I continued to deny my intuition and what was transpiring right in front of my eyes.

All along, I had been claiming truth as one of my relationship values. But now, I questioned if I had evidence to prove it. How did it show up in my behavior? Was I able to speak my truth? Could I ask for the truth? Was I brave enough to hear his truth? I realized my values, words and actions weren't aligned.

Wondering if he just needed a little space, I decided to be patient and not push for an explanation. I had already believed *I was the problem,* and I moved forward with my first therapy appointment one morning that week. And then the truth became my reality.

***

When the appointment ended, one of our dogs came into the room and jumped on the bed to snuggle with me. My session was intense, and I welcomed a little comfort. Brian followed him into the room and sat down on the bed. After we exchanged small talk about the dog, I received the clarity I had been waiting for. It was not what I expected.

"It's time we separate," he said.

I was stunned. *This is what has been going on?* We had some challenges, as most relationships do, but I had assumed they were indicative of the cycle of ups and downs in a long-term relationship. I did not realize we were on the edge of divorce.

"Let's consider therapy," I begged. But it was too late for him.

I was so shocked I didn't know what to say.

"We need to talk more about this."

Since he was on his way to work, he agreed to talk more later. Then he got up to leave.

Devastated and in shock, I stayed in bed and lay there for a while, drowning in a pool of tears.

The follow-up conversation I had been desperate to have was a blur to me. I wanted more substance, something concrete for me to grasp onto. But all I could hear was he was not happy and was looking for a new place to live.

***

A week or so later, it was time to take my finals for my yoga teaching certification program. I spent some time in the early morning contemplating all it took to reach this point on my yoga journey. For a long time, I expected I'd wake up one day and have a feeling inside that spoke clearly to me as a "Yes, teaching is IT and I am ready," but it never arrived.

Instead, I stumbled upon my certification program and went for it. I just stepped into the idea that I could be a teacher. It was this decision that brought me to this point.

But now that the time had arrived for me to step in and show up, I was terrified.

Our finals included teaching a short class to the rest of the cohort. My shit from childhood—self-doubt and fear of failure—came up as I prepared. Memories of starting and stopping gymnastics lessons came forward. I was afraid of the balance beam, of tripping on the vault, of moving through space on the parallel bars. I remembered how insecure I felt about my ability to play piano and guitar well enough to perform to expectations, so I quit those too.

As a kid, I learned to value the gifts of my head over my heart. I was smart. I did all my homework and followed the rules of school: answer the teacher's questions when called on and get a gold star, bring home A's and make my parents proud. So, the yoga finals triggered my wound that created the belief that *love and approval was tied to how well I perform vs. who I am as a person.*

The fear of forgetting a pose, a cue, or an entire sequence on one side of the body sent me into a tailspin. I leaned on my typical strategy for avoiding failure: over-preparation. Every single pose and cue in my sequence was researched and detailed word for word on paper. The night before I had to teach,

I was so anxious that I barely slept. Operating on fumes and reeling from what was going on at home, I reviewed my notes again that morning, studying them for the umpteenth time and fueling up my tired spirit with coffee.

And then suddenly, I was sick of it. The over-preparation was increasing my anxiety. As I looked at my notes, I noticed everything I wrote was already in me. I had embodied it from the experience of practicing yoga for over seventeen years. If I forgot a pose, another would certainly come forward. My attempts to be perfect and avoid failure were making me a wreck. So, I put down the material and sat for a brief meditation. I closed my weary eyes, placed my hands on my heart, and asked Spirit to help me trust myself. I sat for several minutes, calling in my wisdom. When I was done, I grabbed my mala beads for good luck and drove to the yoga studio.

When it was time to teach, my heart was beating out of my chest. I was so nervous; my voice cracked as I guided the group through a breath exercise to begin the class. I didn't forget my sequence because my inner critic worked hard to keep me in check. *Stay focused. Remember. Don't fuck up.* My head was 100% present, delivering rehearsed cues for the poses, but my heart not so much. At this moment, I was OK with that because my mind historically protected me.

When my class was over, a tremendous rush of energy dropped into my body from head to toe, a combination of relief, exhilaration, and exhaustion. It was then that I received a dose of clarity: *Everything I need is already inside of me—all of my knowledge, all of my answers. Listening to and trusting my intuition will guide me in the right direction.*

As I stepped into teaching, I had to practice trusting myself and what I already knew. I had to practice letting go of perfection.

Little did I know this moment of clarity would become the foundational philosophy for how I managed my healing process. Because I was not aware I needed to go on this journey until after my then-partner's departure.

***

When he moved out, he took with him our bedroom furniture. He closed the bedroom door before he left, and I kept it that way for weeks until I felt ready to face the emptiness behind it.

The day I felt courageous, I entered the room. Random trash and other discarded remnants of his life mixed with dust bunnies lay all over the floor. The closet was empty except for what he left behind: a box of documents, hangers, and the vacuum cleaner. All the drawers in the bathroom vanity were open, but not empty. I couldn't help but feel like the state of the room reflected someone who had to bolt. And the mess was mine to clean. Every bone in me refused the task at hand. I simply didn't want to be the one to do it.

Rather than call a cleaning service, I sent a text to a friend who had previously referred a top-notch local housekeeper to me. I needed her name again.

Did you move out?

> *No, he did, and he left behind a mess that I don't want to clean.*

I've wondered how things were going.

What do you mean?

In the next few messages, she shared her perspective on my marriage. As I read them, I could feel a heaviness come over me. I was already in shock from his move and now I was standing in our empty bedroom for the first time. I called another girlfriend for additional support afterwards, and she took the opportunity to share her perspective with me, too. After we talked, I realized their perspectives seemed similar—and they were the opposite of mine.

Since my world was already upside down, hearing other people's views on my marriage led me to question my reality. *Did I truly know him? Did I know myself? Did I trust myself? What was real?* When I couldn't come up with answers, it crushed me to realize I had placed my hopes and dreams in the fairytale of marriage.

***

I had an amazing support system during this time, but the more I talked about what I was going through, the less helpful it was. The shock I felt left a deafening emptiness inside of me, and nothing anyone could say could heal that. I retreated instead, preferring solitude over support.

I spent many nights lying in silence or in tears, just being with this emptiness. Convinced I had missed red flags in our relationship, I continued digging through the past to see if I could find them. But the searching and rumination weren't helping me find the answer to the question that felt natural to ask: *Who was to blame?*

I questioned myself. I doubted my judgment and wondered if I was as smart and enlightened as I thought I was. I struggled with believing others had the answers I was looking for, not realizing I was looking outside myself to heal the confusion and pain I felt inside.

My already-heavy heart sank the day I received a screenshot of a social media post that hinted at the possibility of a new woman in his life three months after he moved out. That wasn't all. Because of that social media post, what was going on for me privately was now news to a wider network of friends.

The humiliation I felt grew stronger, and all I wanted to do was hide.

What hurt the most was the sense of betrayal I felt. I called my mom one night in tears and said, "Why did he ask me to marry him?" I had to come to terms with the fact that he was just not my person. This was just one of the messages the Universe had for me.

***

How you choose to walk through the fire matters, and somehow, I knew I would not burn. A part of me knew I would be the one to forge my path through it and pull myself out.

For a while, I sat with all the shock, confusion, sadness, and humiliation. I let these emotions marinate within me, not trying to change them or make them go away. The longer they marinated, the more I noticed I was quietly being invited into an inquiry: *What had prevented me from wanting to see this relationship as anything other than how I saw it?*

This is when my healing journey began.

It was curiosity—not blame or rumination—that opened up possibilities for me. It helped me widen my vision and explore the territory. As I stayed open and searched for answers, I was able to see I was the one breaking my heart. I learned healing from this time in my life was a multilayered journey, one that happened little by little. Like the ocean waves of grief, it ebbed and flowed. What follows is the wisdom I gained from curiously and intuitively guiding myself back towards myself—the lessons through which I eventually met my Brave Wise Woman.

At the end of each lesson, I invite you into a simple practice related to the topic. Each practice is intended to open up new possibilities within you on your healing path. A journal isn't necessary, but it can be helpful for capturing your reflections and insights. As a companion to the practices, amplify your healing further with *8 Powerful Intentions to Awaken Your Brave Wise Woman*. To access your free copy, visit www.bravewisewoman.com.

II

Wisdom From Within

Lesson 1

Call on Your *Medicines* to Support You

"You're braver than you believe, stronger than you seem and smarter than you think."

- Christopher Robin from Winnie-the-Pooh by A. A. Milne

Reclaiming our life and identity after a major breakup can feel disorienting, raw, and tender. Sometimes, we end up believing the stories we tell ourselves—the ones that have us convinced we *lack*. What if you knew that instead of *lacking*, you are already gifted inside with a mix of special qualities that can fully support your healing path?

Realizing these qualities begins by choosing a path of trust and compassion. We become more aware of our innate wholeness when we embark on a journey of discovering who we are. As multidimensional beings, we are never lacking. Our life experiences reveal our layers—some dark, some light. As we meet these new layers, we are simultaneously being invited to evolve by embracing what is revealed to us, even when it's challenging. Compassion for our sometimes-messy path and our humanness helps us do that.

That being said, when we're hurting, we encounter moments in which it's difficult to see how we'll make it through. Sometimes even compassion—a much-needed ally on our healing path—can feel elusive. As humans, we seek pleasure and try to avoid pain. We will do anything to avoid it: watch TV, scroll on our phones, stay busy, shop, eat, drink, and use substances. Admittedly, it feels good sometimes to have a temporary diversion from the heaviness. Long term though, we can block ourselves from the healing process and, ultimately, the life experiences we desire for ourselves.

Our ability to cope in difficult times is our resilience. The Merriam-Webster Dictionary defines resilience as "an ability to recover from or adjust easily to misfortune or change." It's how we get through tough times and bounce back, hopefully stronger and wiser than we once were. I believe all of our experiences teach us about our resilience. We learn how to navigate the waves and trust them. We learn to be resourceful. Some of our support resources exist outside of us, such as our network of close friends and family we lean on or professional healers. But others come from our wholeness; they live within us.

We are all gifted with inner qualities that we can consciously draw on to support our healing journey. You can think of them as positive attributes, or you can think of them as medicines. Sand Symes, a modern medicine woman and coach, taught me about the power of thinking about these attributes as medicines. "Medicines" gives them a different frequency, one that we can consciously use as a positive force in our life to support us. They can help us with our responses to difficult moments and change. Tony Robbins, author and coach, often says, "Life doesn't happen to you, it happens *for you.*" It may not feel that way sometimes, especially while in the throes of making sense of your life, but this perspective invites us into possibility: If this difficult moment is happening *for* you, which of your medicines could you consciously call on to support your healing?

We can observe these inner qualities— our medicines—in our successes or in how we consistently interact with the world. Authenticity, kindness, fairness, honesty, creativity, and generosity—whatever we have inside of us—can be called on in difficult times to help us through. It's a shift in perspective and mindset. Sometimes we might not think we have certain attributes, but if we can witness them in other people, they exist inside of us as well. All relationships are mirrors, reflecting back to us who we are.

Three of my specific medicines emerged organically as those that would form the foundation for this leg of my healing journey. Perhaps they exist in you as well.

Curiosity

Curiosity is an innate quality we are all born with. Think back to when you were a child. Everything in your world was new. You crawled and explored. You touched things and stared at your fingers; you were curious. I developed this medicine, this strength of mine, early on. My favorite word as a kid was *why*. None of my questions were simple for my mother to answer. I met each answer with a *why*.

I heard Britt Frank, trauma specialist, therapist, and author, say on a podcast, "The step in between judging ourselves and loving ourselves is curiosity." This quality is more than a medicine; it's a bridge to self-love. It implies we can interrupt patterns of negative self-criticism and invite new perspectives. As an adult, I have never stopped asking *why*, and once I turned my curiosity inward, it helped me go deeper. I learned *why* I am the way I am, *why* my parents are the way they are, *why* I enter relationships, and *why* all of it contributed to the fallout of my marriage.

Faith

Faith is something we can't see; we can only ever experience faith through trust. While I'm not a person of religious faith, I had a strong sense early on that the ending of my marriage served a greater purpose. It was happening *for* me. When the pain was overwhelming, I called on the medicine of faith, trusting that through this dark moment in my life, the Universe was delivering a positive transformative experience. I knew I had to trust it.

Whatever you believe to be true can have a powerful impact on your life. Our beliefs underpin our outcomes. You *can* overcome the difficult moment, survive the emotional rollercoaster, and be a better person because of it. Having faith will help you get there and help you align your response with the moment.

Patience

I stayed with my mom the week after Brian notified me that he had found a new apartment. While I was there, she convinced me to consult with a divorce lawyer. Given how shocked I was, it felt too early and overwhelming for me. But I agreed anyway.

His words were succinct, "In the years I've been doing this, [I've seen that] if you don't know the truth about why your marriage ended, be patient. The truth always comes out."

The invitation was to call on patience as a medicine and let the process unfold naturally. This is an example of a quality I don't consider to be a clear strength, but I witness it in other people, so it exists in me too. I couldn't see another option but to accept the invitation to practice patience. And in doing so, I could build up my patience muscle.

As we come to know new layers of who we are, additional medicines are called forward to support our progress along our healing journey.

An Invitation to Call Your Medicines Forward

I invite you to identify your inner medicines and consciously draw on them to support your healing journey. They are as unique as you are.

Bring to mind some of the positive experiences in your life. They could be successes such as those at work, at home, with other people, or moments in your life that felt powerful and true to you. Reflect on the following questions as journal prompts:

- What qualities or traits are present in those experiences?

- What themes can you see?

Think of someone that you admire, regardless of whether you know them personally. What are you drawn to in that person? What traits do you most admire? Is it their tenacity? Their compassion? Their wisdom? Add your thoughts to your list. We can witness in others the traits that exist within us. You may not think you possess these now, but through practice and experience, you can build your confidence in them.

Now, invite the wisdom of your body to assist in helping you pick two to three medicines to call forward to support your situation. You might notice a somatic response as you reflect on the qualities on your list one at a time. What sensations are present? Where are they located? Do they have a texture, color or image? Which medicines resonate the most? Now, select those you'd like to bring into your conscious awareness. How can you envision them supporting you?

The Takeaway

Our difficult moments invite us into a new relationship with ourselves, and we face a choice about how we want to navigate them. One belief that can prevent us from connecting with the wisdom of our true self as we heal is: "I am not resourceful." Another is, "Life happens *to* me." The truth is we all have what we need, and our answers are inside of us, always. When we embrace the possibility that the challenge we're experiencing right now is painful but might ultimately be *for* us, we can show up for the moment more empowered. Our positive qualities and attributes—the medicines already inside of us— can be our most valuable allies, serving as internal North Stars along the way.

Lesson 2

Breathe. Heal. Now.

"The next message you need is always right where you are."

- Ram Dass

One of the most challenging parts of navigating a relationship ending is dealing with what our mind puts us through. We are rarely in the present moment because we're too busy replaying the past or freaking out about the future—or avoiding the pain of it altogether. Bouncing between our memories and fear and anxiety can be overwhelming and exhausting. But we have another medicine within us we can call on as an ally: the breath.

What You Can Control

Throughout the day, we breathe without thinking much about it. But it is also the only body system we can control. We both *allow* the breath to be passive and can consciously turn to it to support us. The breath hints at our internal state. When it's fast and shallow, anxiety, fear, or stress might be present, which indicates an activated sympathetic nervous system signaling danger or a fight-or-flight response. By elongating our exhales, we can activate our parasympathetic nervous system and induce more relaxation. This is comforting to me because it means we have a tool available at our fingertips 24/7. When we connect with the breath, we connect to what's happening in front of us right now. We connect to what's real.

But because humans naturally want to feel pleasure and avoid pain, many of us distract ourselves. We stay busy or avoid feeling our emotions through numbing activities. Healing from a major relationship ending doesn't happen when we're distracted by doing, by knocking tasks off our to-do list. It doesn't happen when we're feeling fear and freaking out about how we will rebuild our life, nor does it happen by replaying all the ways we could have shown up differently. It happens in the present moment. The breath is a tool that can help us access it.

It Doesn't Have to Be Meditation

People either love meditation or have a hard time getting into it. I'm part of the latter group. I've been working on mindfulness for a long time through my yoga practice, but seated meditation can be super challenging for me. When I sit, I can witness my mind steamrolling through. You might ask, "Well, isn't the point to witness it?" And to that I say, "Yes, that's *one* reason to practice, to witness it."

From breathwork to visualization methods, there are a vast number of practices to choose from. Some work with a central focal point, such as a light or breath, or through movement. But I believe meditation can take the shape of whatever set of practices we choose. We can freestyle our own experience as long as it brings us into the present and invites us to drop our attention away from our mind and into our breath and other wisdom centers—our heart and body.

Through my yoga practice, I've learned a lot about mindfulness and my breath. One of the most memorable moments happened while I was in class. I was in downward dog pose when the teacher got down on his knees to whisper, "An advanced yogi softens her breath." I had been breathing like Darth Vader on the mat for seven years, so I was put off by his comment at first. But then I got curious.

What did he mean?

It took some trial and error, but I eventually realized I had been trying to prove something on the mat, to myself and others around me. My ego was present and showing itself in the quality of my breath: forceful and loud. So, I experimented with what it felt like to soften it, and when I found the balance between effort and ease, my yoga practice was renewed. I moved with more fluidity and presence. It also helped build my self-awareness muscle off the mat. I understand now that *allowing* invites us to *receive* what we need, whether on or off the mat.

But this experience didn't translate for me in a seated meditation practice. I believed the point was to have no thoughts while meditating, but I had them all the time! I'd start off focused but would quickly notice my active mind, then breathe more forcefully in an attempt to control it while judging myself for it. Frustration would set in because I didn't believe I was doing it right. I didn't trust the process. So, I gave up.

But a daily meditation practice was a requirement in my yoga teacher training certification program. My resistance was apparent right away in how I tried to control my approach. I made a list of things to do to get started. First, I needed a place to sit, so I set one up. Then I needed the right time of day to do it, so I scheduled it on my calendar. Then I needed a timer. I did not know how long I could tolerate sitting, so I started small: five minutes. I closed my eyes and followed my breath in and out of my body but quickly noticed my mind was off in the future, contemplating what I had to do when the timer went off. I didn't want to be present. Those first five minutes were the longest five minutes ever.

I kept at it, though. Five minutes a day until I could get through five minutes without wishing I was somewhere else. When that became easier, I experimented with increasing my time, first to ten, then fifteen, and finally twenty minutes a day. The longer I'd sit, the more I'd notice my mind bouncing around, taking me to the past or the future, sometimes sending me down a rabbit hole. *What time do I need to be ready by tonight? What am I going to wear? I need coffee for tomorrow. I wonder if I have time to run to the store before I go out.* As soon as I noticed the thought parade, I'd refocus my attention on the breath. It wasn't long before I became antsy. *How long has it been? It feels like forever. Am I almost done yet? Should I look at my phone?* Funny enough, when I'd feel the most fidgety, the timer would sound just a couple of minutes later, and I was always grateful to hear it.

I was often squeezing meditation in between meetings or as something on my to-do list. On paper, I was making progress and like a good student, I was doing what I was supposed to do to fulfill my yoga homework. Was it serving me, though? I continued to question if I was doing it right.

It wasn't until Brian and I separated that my experience shifted.

I was an anxious mess leading up to the day he moved out, then once he left, I felt out of my body. Most of the time, I couldn't put my finger on what I was feeling. I was going through the motions, trying to put one foot in front of the other, but it was like trying to swim in a tub of molasses. Half the time,

I was crying, the other half, I wanted to crawl out of my skin. I was in an unfamiliar place of shock.

Sometimes my corporate job was a welcome distraction for me. I was grateful to work from home most of the time too. But one day, I couldn't find the energy to deal with work. I was so agitated inside that I couldn't sit still and focus. Peering outside the sliding glass doors near my desk, I could see the sun outside on my back porch. The back of the building was a quiet zone. Trees, birds, and squirrels surrounded the property. I decided I needed to be outside.

Leaving my phone on the table, I went onto the back porch and sat on a cushion, closed my eyes, and simply breathed. As I did so, I noticed the warmth of the sun on my face and took in how good it felt at that moment to be nurtured by it. I sat for a while that morning just feeling the sun. Time was not important to me. I just wanted *to be*.

The next day, I returned to the porch at the same time of the day, just to sit, breathe, feel the sun, and hear silence. When I didn't have any motivation to do what I needed to do, I'd return to the same spot to sit. Whenever the energy inside felt overwhelming, I'd sit again. If I was lucky, sometimes I sat more than once per day, being still in the moment and tuning into my senses. The warmth of the sun on my skin, my breath gently moving in and through my body, and the peace surrounding me brought me back into my body. It reminded me *I am.* I often placed my hands on my heart and spoke to myself.

I am here. I am surviving this moment. The Universe has a plan and I trust it. Even if I don't know what it is or what to do, I will be OK.

This routine of tuning into my senses, my breath, and speaking gently to myself became my regular meditation practice.

As a medicine, faith gave me a North Star, a reason to go through the pain because something else awaited me on the other side. But on the most challenging days, when that sense of faith was harder to access, coming into presence on the porch created space for a deep sinkhole of grief to emerge. Each moment, each breath, each tear was deep devastation. As more of these emotional waves emerged in meditation, I realized I was being called to be with what I held inside that desperately needed to be expressed. The invitations gave me permission to feel and release the grief while also surrendering to the experience with compassion. I was learning how to *allow* myself to be with my breath and senses so I could *receive* what I needed most at that moment.

Let it flow. I am OK in my grief. I am surviving this moment.

For six months after he moved out, either my faith was strong or I felt deep grief in my meditation practice. I stayed present with whatever showed up each day, knowing that I would survive the moment.

I trusted what it felt like to allow, receive, and surrender to what my heart needed. My approach to meditation helped me heal.

And my inner critic quieted down, too. She came to find I was doing it right.

An Invitation to Practice Connecting with the Breath

I invite you to explore your breath with curiosity and explore how spending just a few moments with it can influence your presence and change your state. I have a simple mindfulness practice for you to try called the 1:1 breath.

Find a quiet spot where you can spend a couple of minutes without distractions. Try to sit up straight, stacking ears above shoulders, shoulders above hips, and lower belly slightly pulled in. Be comfortable but not too relaxed. If it feels safe for you, close your eyes or soften your gaze. Rest your hands on your belly.

For the first few breath cycles, breathe naturally and notice if you are holding onto any tension in your body. Scan from head to toe and simply notice. Invite any tension to soften as you exhale.

Next, notice your breath moving in and out of your body. Is it fast? Slow? Does it have a temperature? Notice your hands moving along in time with the belly as you breathe.

Now, how many counts is your inhale? What about your exhale?

After you've counted your inhales and exhales for a few breath cycles, breathe a little deeper and lengthen the inhale by one count. If your breath was a three-count breath, now make it four counts.

Then match the length of the exhale with the inhale. If you are inhaling now for four counts, exhale for four.

Breathe here for a few breath cycles. Maybe quietly say a few nurturing words to yourself, such as, "I am safe."

You can explore the experience further by adding another count for each inhale and exhale. Or to induce a calmer state, make the count of your exhales longer than your inhales.

When you feel ready, open your eyes and notice how you feel physically, emotionally, and mentally.

If this practice has resonated, I encourage you to continue doing it as a foundation for your healing.

The Takeaway

As a medicine, the breath is an ally we can call on to facilitate our healing. Through the breath, we can connect to what's right here, right now. We can shift our awareness from outside of us to inside. The more we practice presence, the more we create space to heal, and our capacity to receive what we need from the experience grows. *Allowing* can lead to *receiving*.

When we permit ourselves to design our own approach to cultivating more presence, rather than following the way others are doing it, or approaching it in a way that doesn't work for us, we receive unexpected gifts: the gift of self-discovery and the gift of developing a closer connection with the wisdom of our authentic self.

Want more?

Amplify your healing journey with this companion to the lessons in this book:

8 Powerful Intentions for Awakening Your Brave Wise Woman

Visit www.bravewisewoman.com to receive your gift and join a community of women who will receive exclusive tips and offers for upcoming programs to help you meet your Brave Wise Woman.

Lesson 3

Emotions Are Teachers Too

"No matter the feelings. You can transform the energy of your emotions into your power."

- Matthew Donnelly

Everything in our life is a teacher, including people, choices, and what happens or doesn't happen for us. Every experience reveals to us who we are. Emotions are no different. Happiness can teach us what makes us feel light. Grief can teach us who we love. Anxiety can hint at what we fear.

As a natural part of the human experience, all emotions help us understand and respond to our environment. If we judge our emotions as good or bad, we have likely received direct or indirect messages about them in our childhood from our caregivers or society, and formed beliefs about them, such as *sadness is scary* or *I am bad for being angry.* Since our beliefs drive everything, if we form a belief about our emotional experience based on judgment ("good" or "bad"), we can end up adopting strategies that prevent us from feeling and expressing them. Avoiding or suppressing our emotions denies us of our humanity and causes us to miss out on their gifts—what they can teach us about navigating our world.

***

Anger can be a challenging emotion to own and navigate. In our culture, I believe so few of us have a healthy relationship with it that role models for healthy expression of anger can be hard to come by. The first people we learn from are usually our parents or primary caregivers. What have your parents taught you about anger?

When my parents argued, they would literally and figuratively point their fingers at each other. As a young girl, I could feel the energy in the room grow thick and tense as their voices got louder, and I watched their body language change. When I got into trouble, I was on the receiving end of this energy, and I'd end up in tears before being sent to my bedroom as punishment.

But the belief I formed about anger came from my experience of what occurred afterward in the repair process. When it was time to come out from my bedroom, I'd tentatively approach my father with tears in my eyes. As I stood there eager for reassurance I was still loved, sometimes he would sit there, arms crossed, looking at the television instead of at me, with no facial expression. It could have been seconds or minutes, but time would stand still until he acknowledged my presence. Through this nuance in how he repaired, I adopted the belief *anger is bad because when people are angry with me, love and connection go away.* Because our survival as children is tied to our primary caregivers, this felt like death.

So, I became a good girl who did what she was told. I performed to receive approval (and survive). I was smart and always did my homework. I kept my bedroom tidy and made my bed every morning the minute I got out of it. At bedtime, I'd sit on my pillow and slither under the sheets from the top so I didn't disturb the perfect fold of the sheets over the blankets. My bed was never a mess, even when I slept in it.

I grew up conflict-averse, not wanting to do or say anything to provoke anger in others. I also wasn't taught how to process my anger and don't recall being allowed to express it. I turned it inward, and my inner critic strengthened. I judged or blamed myself for whatever went wrong. For most of my life, I wasn't aware that anger—which I interpreted as "bad" and tried to avoid—actually could be a teacher. But to get there, I had to move through its energy to receive its messages. My first opportunity to learn this arrived after my ex-husband and I split.

***

In the months after he moved out, I had reasons to be angry, including what seemed like an abrupt life change and not fully understanding why we split. But I wasn't allowing myself to feel it. My friends suggested I talk to him, but I was reluctant. Confronting him meant I'd have to face this emotion and potentially hear truths I wasn't ready for. Since I believed *anger was bad*, I learned to deny its presence within me.

"The timing isn't right to talk to him," I'd say. And it wasn't. I simply wasn't ready.

What I didn't truly understand about anger is that it has energy that invites us to express ourselves. But I was holding that energy inside. The day I could no longer contain it, I was in the middle of taking a yoga class. I was having a difficult time moving on the mat. Everything about how my body moved felt laborious; my legs were like anchors. I became more frustrated by the minute. Just as I was transitioning into the next pose, I felt a surge of energy in my belly, and it traveled up to my throat. The energy was so forceful it felt like it could burst out of every pore in my body.

My first instinct was to scream out loud, and it took everything I had not to do that in the middle of class. So, I stopped moving, knelt on the mat, closed my eyes, and tried to navigate the energy through my breath. I could feel the mat underneath me. I could hear the teacher cueing the next pose. But I couldn't escape the internal sensations of fire. My chest felt tight. My heart was pounding. As I focused on my breath, I was able to identify the feelings: at first, frustration, then despondence, and finally, powerlessness.

The energy of anger that was swirling around in my body was now unlocked. Tears rolled down my cheeks as I sat there for several minutes. My two choices were to pick up my stuff and leave the studio or stay. The yoga mat was the one place I felt strong and in control, so I stayed.

I spoke gently to myself. *It's OK, I'm going to be OK.* I took a few more deep breaths while sitting on my mat and then moved into downward dog pose and finished the class.

Now that anger reared its head, it began leaking out of me everywhere. In the days that followed, the emotional energy continued to surface as irritability. Everything and everyone was a source of irritation: the anxiety issues of the dog I got custody of in our separation, stupid drivers on the road, people at work who needed my help, random people who said hello to me on my favorite hiking trail, nice strangers at the grocery store, not-so-nice people too. Anyone around me was literally in my way. I was so irritated!

In his book *Power vs. Force*, David Hawkins, MD, Ph.D. shares findings of his research indicating emotions have an energy that can be measured. When the energy of anger surfaced during a yoga class, and I didn't allow it to completely move through my body, a charge within me remained. I suppressed the energy flow just to finish the class. The energy surfaced again as irritability, a low-level version of anger. Since then, I've learned movement or exercise can be an effective way to move emotional energy up and out of the body. To do that, we have to focus on the feelings and bodily sensations while in motion and allow the body to do what it naturally knows how to do rather than control the experience.

One day, after returning home and walking through the living room, I accidentally bumped into the corner of the dark brown sectional couch Brian and I had shared for many years. We placed it in the middle of the living room, and it was the first thing I saw every time I opened the front door. When I bumped into it that day, it instantly became the target of everything I was feeling inside.

"Get the fuck out of my way!"

I kicked the couch, then paused.

"You asshole! I fucking hate you! I fucking hate you! Get the fuck out of my fucking way! Fuck you. Fuck you! I hate you, you fucking asshole! I fucking hate you!"

I kicked it again. As tears rolled down my face, I kicked it again. And again. And again.

Then I was done. I backed away from the couch, shut off the lights in the living room, and went to bed.

I immediately hated the couch after that. It was a visible reminder of my former life. I wouldn't sit on it and wanted it out of my way. My first approach was to move it into a corner of the room so it wasn't in my face. But it had become a dark, dead weight in the home. Just as we can't shove our emotions aside, moving the couch to the side didn't make it disappear. But when it became my emotional punching bag, it cleared the way for me to receive the message anger had for me.

While sharing this couch story with a friend, he said, "You know, you can always start over. *You can shift the energy.*"

His words quietly gnawed at me, resonating on some level. I sensed a piece of wisdom was brewing for me in the experience and stayed curious. Every time I looked at the living room after that, I realized I was living in the shell of a leftover life I was mourning.

I called a local charity and requested a furniture donation. They happily sent a driver to pick up the media cabinet and area rug. I sold an expensive coffee table for peanuts online. I just wanted it out of the house. A friend bought the couch for her brother. The living room was now empty, but I didn't stop there. I made a second call to donate my guest room's bedroom set. By the time I was done,

I had nothing left except a mattress on the floor, a dining table to work on, and a pile of clothes. All the furniture in the home was gone.

Armed with a small budget, I went shopping not just to replace the basics but to prepare the home for my future situation: a roommate. The first step was moving out of the guest room and into the other bedroom. Transitioning back into the other bedroom was a big deal to me. It had been almost six months since he moved out. One of my teachers, Preston Smiles, often says, "Readiness isn't always a feeling inside, but a decision." I know through experience this is true.

The day the bedroom furniture was to be delivered, I held a small ceremony in the empty bedroom to clear out the old energy. As I lit a stick of palo santo, turned it upside down, and blew out the flame to create smoke, I set the intention of inviting in new, positive energy. I waved the stick around my body, my head, arms, torso, and legs to clear my energy. I walked around the room, fanning the smoke around each corner and crevice while asking Spirit to bless the space. Then I sat on the floor, set the smudge down, closed my eyes, and breathed in the sweet scent. I placed my hands on my heart and called in the courage to claim the space and this new version of my life as mine.

I had finally received anger's message. It was time to embrace my current reality, grab it by the horns, and take responsibility for owning it.

The sound of the doorbell later that day invited excitement. Within an hour, my furniture was set up, and it was time to decorate. I made my bed with new sheets, a new bright mandala duvet cover, and fresh toss pillows. As I placed mismatched lamps on my nightstands, I imagined the bed had a driver and passenger side and decided the driver's side would be mine. I placed my rose quartz crystals on the passenger side nightstand and set an intention of inviting love into my life again someday. And after my clothes were all set up in the closet and put away in my new dresser, I stood in the doorway and took it all in. The vibe I created differed from the first time around in the space. This time, it felt feminine and harmonious.

The cherry on top was the first piece of art I bought for the empty walls. A large painting for sale at my local yoga studio caught my eye. It was an abstract image of a woman with her arms wrapped around herself in a hug, an image bathed in bright color and light. Not only was it stunning, but it spoke deeply to my heart. The price tag was beyond my initial budget, but with each visit to the studio, it became clearer that the painting already belonged to me.

When the artist delivered it to my home, she explained the meaning of the painting, titled "Tree." It was about standing firm in your values and choices.

"I love it," I said. "The painting represents self-love to me."

I hung it up on the first wall visible upon entering the home.

An Invitation to Release Emotional Energy

Many of us have strategies to avoid feeling our emotions. Some of us stay busy, others numb through food, alcohol, television, or shopping, for example. Some deny they have any feelings at all. Mine is to overthink and analyze, to contain the experience in my head rather than my body. Emotions are part of the total human experience and when we cut ourselves off from them, we disconnect from an important part of who we are. The energy builds and intensifies inside of us. It's like trying to shove an inflated balloon down into a pool of water. It just shoots back up when we take our hand off of it. But there's only one way out of our emotions, which is allowing them to move through us. What medicine can you call forward to support you in moving the energy?

Presence connects us to our emotions, and we can often discover the trailhead for them as a sensation in the body. Sitting quietly, place one hand on your heart and one on your belly. Draw your attention inward and inquire, *What am I feeling at this moment?* Then listen. Notice if your body speaks to you as sensations. What are they? Where are they located? Can you describe them further? Can you name the emotion? And does the sensation or emotion have a message for you?

Our bodies are so wise and hold as much wisdom as our minds.

I invite you to release your hand off that blown-up balloon to move the energy through a writing exercise that I found useful.

- **Write a letter.** The letter you are being invited to write is for *your eyes only*. Since you will not send it to anyone, this is an opportunity to express everything you feel inside. Grab a timer, paper, and a pen. (I recommend not using your journal or your computer.) To begin, start by setting yourself up in a sacred space, with no interruptions. Allow yourself space to get in touch with your mind and body. What does that look like for you?

  Set an intention to call forth your feelings and move the energy through writing, then set your timer for ten minutes. Let it all come out, the sadness, the disappointment, the anger, the grief. Whatever you want to say to someone else or even to yourself, write it out on paper and let the words flow. Don't worry about perfection, spelling, punctuation, or grammar—and feel free to swear! When you are done, *don't read it* (and don't send it.) Let the energy of what was written be released from your system. Rip it up or burn it.

Tip: If it is challenging to connect to your feelings, take a few minutes before you do this exercise to sit in silence with your eyes closed (if it feels safe to do so), and revisit the memory of the experience you are working through. Remembering details can often bring forward the lingering emotion.

The Takeaway

My experience with anger was another example of how *allowing* can lead to *receiving*. By allowing my body to cycle through the emotional experience, I released the energy and created space to receive the message that it was time to step into the reality of my new life and own it. Allowing the energy to express and move is how we get to the other side of emotions. In doing so, we reveal another layer of our humanness and take another step closer to meeting our authentic self.

Cultivating a healthy relationship with our emotions starts by getting out of our heads and into our bodies. Awareness, permission, and compassion can be medicines for the emotional experience.

Awareness is about recognizing you are feeling something, typically starting with sensations in the body. Emotions share a connection with the body, and research was published in 2013 by Finnish researcher Lauri Nummenmaa and his team that mapped the mind-body connection across a range of emotions. You can notice your own mind-body connection with some attention and awareness.

Permission is about allowing yourself to feel as you do and letting it come forward, even if it's uncomfortable, and even if you've received messages in your childhood that it's not OK to have that feeling. Repressing emotions can give them more energy and make them more intense or influence our overall well-being, sometimes turning into other physical symptoms, such as illness or disease. Can you permit yourself to lean into the discomfort and disconnect from any stories you might have about emotions so you can experience the full range of your humanness? Sometimes it's helpful to say, *Feeling this is really challenging. But I'm going to be OK.*

Compassion is not judging yourself for your feelings. Owning your experience with emotions, such as anger or sadness, calls for courage. But if we judge ourselves for how we feel, we unknowingly create the conditions for the emotional energy to linger. Befriending ourselves in a challenging, emotional moment expands our resilience, and gently nudges the door open to receive the messages our emotions have for us. Be soft in the heart with yourself.

I'm safe. It's OK. Let it flow. Let it out.

NOTE: For those dealing with anger issues related to trauma or abuse, I encourage you to work with a trauma specialist. If the hard feelings are too challenging to overcome, enlist the help of a professional.

Lesson 4

Relationships Show Us Who We Are

"Do the best you can, until you know better. Then when you know better, do better."

- Maya Angelou

Have you ever looked back on your romantic history? Or have you buried your past out of embarrassment or shame? Is your pattern to move on to the next lover quickly, or do you take the time to explore lessons learned from your last one?

Whatever your experience is in relationships, they are valuable learning containers, always mirroring back to us what we are consciously and unconsciously bringing to them: our history, our childhood wounds, our energy. If we don't know the crevices of who we are, our relationships will inevitably show us.

What I thought I brought to my relationships was a strong sense of who I was. Smart. Strong. Loving. Capable of figuring out how to do things and doing them well. I was diligent about how I showed up, loyal, and believed I had a desire to do what was right for myself and my romantic partners. I made assumptions that my relationships could thrive because of these qualities. After yet another failed relationship, I questioned if this was true. What was my track record as a romantic partner? Was I as capable as I thought of having a thriving relationship?

I had a habit of ignoring my romantic past. I buried each relationship ending underneath the start of another, refusing to look back. For most of my life, I wasn't aware that relationships were mirrors and teachers. I just moved on to the next one while skipping the part about asking what I learned *about myself* from the last one. A part of me always knew something was off in my relationships, but the shame and embarrassment led me to hide it rather than look at it. The ending of my marriage forced me to take a closer look.

As I snuggled on the couch with my dog, a glass of wine, and a box of tissues, I called on the medicines of courage and permission to go back in time and look at some of my prior relationships.

***

I remembered the fun I had with a boyfriend decades ago, and fun usually involved hanging out at local bars. When we met, I had just ended a two-year phase of going to nightclubs every weekend, so this kind of relationship kept that party spirit alive. And at that time, this was the type of relationship that suited me. I was more interested in checking out and finding someone to love me while doing so. And under the influence, anything can look rosy.

During this relationship, I found yoga. The practice called me to it from the start. I used to think yoga was for people who don't work out, and it took several people telling me to go try it before I reluctantly agreed. From the first class, I was hooked and began taking three classes a week. I had been practicing for six months when one night, while I was sitting on my balcony at home after class, I had a nudge inside about what yoga was all about: learning how to love who I am.

I promptly went back into the house, called my then-boyfriend, and broke up with him. The party had to end.

This moment could have been a powerful teacher, if I had been ready. It could have introduced the question: Is loving myself *just* about a romantic relationship? It could have led me to see the sacrifices I was making just to feel loved.

Instead, I moved on to the next guy. We had interesting conversations and seemed to get along well. I enjoyed our time together.

A couple of months after we met, he surprised me with a proposal. It thrilled him when I accepted, but when I told my parents, they were not as pleased. They had not met him yet. I tried to convince them I was making a sound decision. But the more they pushed back, the more I dug in and defended my choice.

It didn't take long for the Universe to hint as to why taking the time to get to know ourselves and our partners is useful before making a major commitment.

On an international trip, he couldn't find his passport. He panicked as he rummaged through the hotel room looking for it.

"When was the last time you saw it?"

I was panicking along with him. I had no inner tools or awareness at this time in my life. My questions were not helping in the way I assumed they would and he left our room. As I followed him out to try and calm him down, I noticed that tactic wasn't working. At the time, I didn't understand the nature of triggers—an intense reaction to a situation because it unconsciously reminds us of past pain. I now understand my panic was not about the passport, but about my discomfort with the energy of the situation. Unconsciously, I was reacting to the energy I felt from my parents when they argued. I was trying to make it stop.

After some time, we returned to our room and found the passport. A part of me was relieved. Another part of me wondered, *What just happened?*

As time went on, it became clear I did not know how to communicate well. I couldn't handle arguments. My go-to tactic was to use logic or attempt to calm things down. Being conflict-averse, eventually I shut down inside. Rather than talk about it with close friends, I kept it all inside.

One night, entangled in a heated argument resulting in tears, I blurted the only words that I could think of to end it. "I don't love you!" As soon as the sound of *ooo* in "you" came out of my mouth, I knew I was free. My knees wobbled, and all the energy in my body fell to my feet. I was terrified because I didn't want to continue feeling the way I did and I lacked the maturity to know any other way to make that happen.

After he moved out, I built my life back up little by little. I took my rent money and bought a mattress to put on the floor. Gift certificates from my mom helped me replace dishes and other necessities. But material goods were no cure for the guilt that followed in the aftermath. It was true I didn't love him anymore. But another truth simmered inside.

As a good girl, I knew accepting a marriage proposal a few months into dating was out of character for me. But I didn't know who I was yet. I said yes because I didn't love myself enough to speak my truth.

Betraying another person is hard enough. Saying yes when your intuition tells you a *no* or *not right now* response feels more appropriate is self-betrayal, and facing my self-betrayal felt like a special hell. I spent the months that followed sitting on an empty stereo box at night under an open window, cruelly beating myself up while smoking cigarettes, drinking wine, and crying until my eyes were shut. I kept all of this to myself as I had during this relationship because I did not want anyone else to know how shitty a person I believed I was. This is how shame breaks down your spirit.

Six months later, I was dating Brian.

What I believed about Brian was that if I was ever in danger, he was the type of man who would save me. I trusted he would know how to get hard things done in life, such as find me in a hospital if I was in an accident. This was a worst-case scenario, of course, but it comforted me to believe he could be that man. So, when he proposed five years later, I said yes because I felt I had met my person.

As I reflected on my relationship with him, I realized that at a macro-level, his presence represented security—a security I had not known yet in my life, not from my father, not from anyone else I had dated, and not within myself. This awareness helped me understand why I buried my head in the sand when our marriage was dying and ending. I was unconsciously choosing to ignore, to give us the benefit of the doubt, because of *what I needed*, which was to continue to feel a sense of security.

As soon as I pulled the decisions made in my romantic past out of the shadows and into the light, I questioned what I believed about love, what the role of partnership means to me, and how I truly felt about myself. The belief I had about relationships came into view. *Having someone to love me* was the goal; like an accomplishment. It wasn't about being a real partner to someone. Unconsciously, I was yearning *to be chosen*, and to be chosen, I believed I needed to abandon myself in small and big ways, including by people-pleasing, ignoring my intuition and not advocating for myself. The quest to *be chosen* prevented me from meeting myself sooner and from learning what I needed to learn to help me grow. At the time, I was not aware this stemmed from a childhood wound I was unconsciously trying to heal. But it was clear I had not yet met my Brave Wise Woman.

An Invitation to Review Your Romantic Past

I invite you into your own version of a relationship audit with the goal of unearthing patterns. Here are a few questions to consider as you reflect on each relationship. Others might emerge as you journal the responses.

- Why did you enter that relationship?
- How did you communicate together?

- What, if anything, did you believe you had to sacrifice to be in the relationship?

- What did that relationship teach you about yourself?

As you do this exercise, it's helpful to call in self-compassion as a medicine. We make decisions in our lives based on what we know at the time. And we learn what we need to know next when the time arrives for us to know it.

The starting point for healing any pattern is to bring awareness to it. If you spot a pattern as you review your answers, ask yourself, *Is this pattern still serving you?*

Seeing where our romantic patterns come from starts by looking more closely at our childhood experiences, which is the topic embedded in the next lesson.

The Takeaway

Looking at our romantic history and getting real with ourselves about our choices and patterns is a necessary part of learning how to love who we are. When we use our medicine of courage to uncover our truth and examine it, the energy of whatever we might hide because of embarrassment or shame releases because we bring it into the light. Our courage helps us peel back another layer so we can begin to connect with our most authentic self.

I believe readiness is everything: for doing this work, for seeing patterns you hadn't noticed before, and for making the invisible visible. We make choices with the knowledge we have. The Universe will always deliver what you need to know when it is time to consider choosing differently. Like waves, our insights ebb and flow as we grow and evolve. Give yourself grace and compassion as you go.

NOTE: If you've experienced trauma or abuse in your relationships, I encourage you to work with a trauma specialist.

Want more?

Amplify your healing journey with this companion to the lessons in this book:

8 Powerful Intentions for Awakening Your Brave Wise Woman

Visit www.bravewisewoman.com to receive your gift and join a community of women who will receive exclusive tips and offers for upcoming programs to help you meet your Brave Wise Woman.

Lesson 5

The Past Is Driving Your Present

"I am out with lanterns, looking for myself."

- Emily Dickinson

O ur behavior is driven by what we're aware of and what is not in our immediate awareness. In our childhood, we are exposed to situations, behaviors of others (such as our primary caregivers), and other environmental factors that influence the beliefs we form, and therefore, the choices we make as adults. Sometimes we have memories of the most influential moments and sometimes we don't, or the link to who we are today is not immediately obvious. If we want to understand and unwind our unhelpful patterns and know ourselves more deeply, we can look to our past for clues.

Reviewing my romantic history was a great start, but I hadn't looked deep enough yet. The golden insight of this work was where the source of my patterns came from. Why *those* specific men? What are the connections with my past? As the saying goes, "Don't blame a clown for acting like a clown. Ask yourself why you keep going to the circus."

Sitting in my meditation space, I opened my journal and wrote the names of the men I had been in relationships with. I jotted down facts, and any other memories I could recall, about them and our time together. I was looking for themes.

At first, I could only see differences in jobs, looks, personal interests, and personalities. Clearly, I didn't have a specific "tall, dark, and handsome" type that I went for, but I stayed the course. I was convinced the men I dated shared commonalities. After an hour, I finally saw what it was—each man on my list had a difficult relationship with their father. I also noticed some had what I perceived to be addictive behavior patterns,[1] such as with cigarettes or alcohol. I added to the list a few men I met after my divorce and no surprises there. Their profiles looked similar.

To see the link between them come to life on paper was huge. I half-jokingly said to myself, "Holy shit. Clearly, more men than we think have a challenging relationship with their father!"

But the common thread was me. I did too.

---

1   I am not a licensed psychologist or therapist. These are my personal opinions shared based on my experiences.

Father Wound

The most fundamental of human needs is to be seen, heard, and understood. What happens when we don't receive what we need most from our parents? Likely, we end up with a wound. The perception of an absence of love and connection (emotional, physical, or both) from a parent or primary caregiver can do that.

As a young girl, I craved connection with my father. Every morning before work, he used to get up early, put on his green terry cloth robe, and head to the kitchen for coffee, a cigarette, and a crossword puzzle while the rest of us slept. Sometimes, I'd hear him and would wake up early just to go visit with him in the kitchen.

"What are you doing out of bed?" he'd ask, the first words of his day. His voice was morning soft yet roughened by the smoke of his cigarette.

I'd crawl up onto a chair at the table and sit with him while he continued with his crossword puzzle. I remember these quiet moments together, few words exchanged. But I also remember yearning for more in those moments with him.

Later in the day, my siblings and I would stand at our big living room window and watch for the car to pull up into the driveway. "Daddy's home!" we'd say as Dad walked up the front steps in his brown uniform. He'd walk in, say hello, pop open a can of beer, and sit on the couch to watch TV. This was his nightly ritual.

If we wanted affection or attention when he came home, we had to go to him. The blue-striped loveseat in our living room wasn't big enough for all of us. My dad was not a small man, but he had not yet gained the amount of weight that eventually contributed to his health issues and the end of his life. So, my sister and I would sometimes fight over who got to sit with him and snuggle up against his sometimes bare, hairy chest and beer belly. I remember being bummed when it wasn't my turn.

My father was not like some dads I know today: the dad who coaches his kid's soccer team and who actively engages in his child's imaginary world. My father wasn't great at building our confidence and was not intimate with our inner lives as we became teenagers. Cognitively, I knew he loved me and was proud of me, but a felt sense of love and approval was missing. In small and big ways, his inability to connect with me emotionally left a scar on my heart. But like a good girl, I kept on trying to forge a closer bond. Occasionally, we'd share moments when I felt like *maybe this will be the time it all turns around and we get closer*, but they were never sustainable. He never really knew all of me before he died.

While he was alive, I tried to understand why my father was the way he was. He had limitations that I couldn't wrap my head around. After his death, I reached a point in my healing when I became interested in my father's relationship with his father. When I did, I was able to see more clearly how his past influenced who he was, and how he parented.

My Father's Wound

My grandfather and my father did not have a close relationship. My dad shared with me that when he was growing up, my grandfather questioned my dad's ability to make something of his life. This left a scar on my father's heart and I suspect he formed the belief he was *not good enough*.

As I dug into my family history to understand more about his childhood, I learned my dad grew up in a home where his parents didn't actively engage with their children's lives. My aunt recalls they didn't ask how school was and what they did. Feelings were not openly discussed either. Some of this may have been cultural. My father was born in the Philippines and migrated to the United States with his family when he was five years old. It might also have been influenced by the professional pressures my grandfather faced once he settled the family here.

My grandpa had built a name for himself as an architect in the Philippines. When he migrated over, his credentials were not acceptable here, and he had to start over at the bottom, as a draftsman initially, then as a licensed building designer for several years until he could earn his architecture license. He focused on reestablishing his career while trying to feed a family of five children, by that time. My grandmother worked as a nurse.

As a young teen, my father excelled in baseball. His middle school team won the city championship. But as I understand it, the family rarely saw him in action. I learned my father spent a lot of time away from the house in his teens and engaged little with the family. My aunt recalls my father would come home late at night and argue with my grandpa when he did.

When my parents announced they had eloped, my grandpa wasn't pleased. According to my mom, he said, "What are you going to support her with, your balls?" My father was twenty-one years old.

I believe my father held onto a lot of anger that stemmed from his childhood. I always felt the energy of anger in my father. It was with him his entire life, sitting inside. Each heartbreak, each personal disappointment, piled one on top of the other. Thirty years after my parents' divorce, and long after he had remarried, anger was still palpable in his voice whenever we would talk about that time in his life. Just as we can become addicted to substances, we can also become addicted to emotional states. This topic is covered in Dr. Joe Dispenza's book *Breaking the Habit of Being Yourself*. I truly believe anger was my father's addiction, and he self-soothed with food.

Knowing more about my father's childhood experiences helped me understand why he had difficulty with emotional connections. Without examples of healthy emotional modeling around him, his anger didn't have an outlet, and my perception was that he became disconnected from himself. Expecting a connection with someone who is disconnected from themselves is like expecting a lightbulb to work when the power has been turned off.

***

Why I kept showing up at the same circus was becoming clearer. Our experiences lead us to unconsciously seek what is familiar. What is familiar to us is attractive because it's comfortable.

My father was my first relationship with a member of the opposite sex. As a hetero woman, my relationship with him as a child molded my perception of what a love relationship ought to look and feel like. I was exposed to the impact of his unhealed wounds, which manifested as a perception of emotional unavailability to me, and I formed a belief based on what I made it mean: *I am not good enough to receive the love, connection, and approval I crave.* That belief has underpinned my romantic partner choices and my behaviors in a relationship. Why? Because I had not done the inner work yet to bring awareness to my wounds and patterns. Instead, I unconsciously recreated them with my partners in an attempt to heal the original relationship dynamic with my father. The unconscious, inner dialogue sounds like this:

> *Maybe this time, I will be seen and validated.*
>
> *Maybe this time, I'll get the love or approval I've been wanting.*
>
> *Maybe this time… with this person, I will be good enough.*

Because our first experience and model of what love looks like comes from our parents or primary caregivers, what we received (or didn't receive) from them becomes an unconscious blueprint for what we seek in our partners. Our partners reflect back what needs to be healed within us.

Attachment Theory

Just after I had the insight into my relationship with my father, I read the book *Attached* by Amir Levine, M.D., and Rachel S.F. Heller, M.A. Attachment theory, and how it manifests in adults, is a massive topic. I encourage you to research it further if you want to understand more about it. Below, I summarize the way I think about the four main attachment styles. Learning about my attachment pattern helped me understand my relationship patterns. It also gave me a new jumping-off point to be curious about.

According to the authors, "attachment theory is based on the assertion that the need to be in a close relationship is embedded in our genes." We are all born with survival instincts and a need for security, connection and belonging. By the time we are about eighteen months old, we develop attachment patterns, or styles, that form the basis for how we bond with our primary caregivers. Attachment patterns are a response to the quality of our parental caregivers' emotional attunement, or connection, to our needs. This becomes the initial blueprint for how we connect in our relationships as adults.

- **Secure:** Children who develop a secure attachment likely have caregivers who are consistently attuned to their needs, responsive, and know how to repair quickly. This lays the foundation for the child to have confidence to explore their world because they trust their caregivers will be there for them. They feel safe and reassured by them. As adults, those with this style tend to have an easier time connecting with others and are comfortable developing intimacy in relationships.

- **Avoidant:** Children who develop an avoidant attachment style tend to have parents who met their basic survival needs such as food and shelter, but may have been emotionally distant or were unable to respond appropriately to the child's other needs. They may have also discouraged displaying emotions. In response, the child learns to become independent. As adults, those with an avoidant attachment style may want a relationship but vulnerability and intimacy can be challenging for them because it feels unsafe. They may keep their relationships at a surface level and pull away when their partner desires more emotional closeness.

- **Anxious**: Children who develop an anxious attachment style tend to have caregivers who are inconsistent with them. One minute they are sensitive to their emotional needs, the next, not. They don't know what to expect from their caregivers. As adults, those with an anxious attachment pattern desire closeness from their partners because closeness equates to safety. They can be hypersensitive to small changes in another's behavior, which trigger their fear of abandonment and drive them to want extra reassurance from others.

- **Disorganized**: A disorganized attachment style typically develops in children who are abused or neglected. The child's caregivers are both a source of safety—they need to get their basic survival needs met through them—and a source of fear. The child desires closeness from their caregivers but because they also fear them, they can reject it. So disorganized attachment is a bit of both avoidant and anxious attachment behavior. As adults, those with this attachment style might want a relationship but, because they've experienced hurt and rejection from their caregivers, may have more difficulty trusting in relationships.

As I learned about the different attachment styles, I recognized my pattern as anxious. This helped me view my romantic patterns in a new light. Since *having someone to love me* was my unconscious goal, it explained why I quickly entered relationships and may have stayed in some beyond their expiration date. It shed light on why I value emotional intimacy as much as I do. It also helped me understand why the end of my marriage devastated me: my fear of abandonment came true.

As I reflected, I realized I had been repeatedly choosing men with wounds similar to my father's to complete the attempt at fostering a close emotional bond and healing the dynamic with my dad. Subconsciously, I believed forming this bond with other men would provide the security and approval I had always longed for in my father.

I understand now that when men with childhood wounds similar to those of my father don't take responsibility for their healing, they are likely unavailable for the emotional depth I'm seeking. I also suspect my father's attachment pattern was avoidant. So my relationships with wounded men with avoidant attachment patterns repeated the cycle of abandonment I fear.

Intergenerational Influences

At various points in my life, I've been bitter toward my parents for their shortcomings and what they couldn't give me. I criticized them because I believed *parents should know better. Why can't my father be the father I want him to be? Why is my mother like that?* From what I could see on the surface, I had no obvious clues. I grew up with a roof over my head, clothes on my back, and food on my table.

When I read about attachment theory, it opened the door for a new level of inquiry. I looked at not just what I could remember, but what wasn't immediately visible to me. I turned my complaints about my parents into questions: *What was behind their inconsistency? What did they learn about parenting?* To answer that, I had to zoom out again. Our parents or primary caregivers have an impact on shaping who we are as adults. And their parents and their history had the greatest impact on who they became.

I already knew about my father's childhood. What about my mother?

She grew up in a home with a father who experienced double trauma in his life. As a soldier in World War II, he had killed a Japanese man to save his own life. According to my grandmother, he returned from the war a changed man. After he came home, my grandfather was diagnosed with a brain tumor and physically recovered.

Afterwards, my grandfather had issues with rage. My mother recalls he once threw his entire tool set down the basement stairs in response to my grandmother asking him to fix what he was repairing for her in a different way. So, my mother grew up in a home where anger was unpredictable and situations escalated. In an attempt to control his behavior, I understand my grandmother used the brain tumor as a scapegoat. I learned she didn't want the kids to talk at the dinner table "because of the brain tumor." They had to leave him alone after work "because of the brain tumor." My mother learned to limit her interactions with her father out of fear.

Both of my parents grew up in homes where meaningful conversations with their families of origin were scarce. I believe my grandparents may not have had the tools to encourage my parents to explore their emotions.

By the time my parents met, I believe they weren't feeling the love and connection they needed at home, so soon after they met on a ski trip, they eloped. Marriage was their escape, a way to fill a perceived void inside. My mom was eighteen years old.

What they each brought to their marriage was an inability to communicate in a healthy way and to have meaningful conversations.

In his book *It Didn't Start with You*, author Mark Wolynn writes, "Perhaps your mother carried a wound from her mother and was unable to give you what she didn't get. Her parenting skills would be limited by what she didn't receive from her parents." What he is saying is that patterns and the impact of wounds are passed down from generation to generation. And my parents unconsciously passed down the impact of their pain to me in their parenting and in what they taught me about love and communication.

With this knowledge, the inquiry I then faced was, *How can I expect my parents to teach me how to love myself if they don't know how to do that for themselves?* My parents were parents to me before they were truly adults. When I saw the total picture and understood their childhood experiences and the people they were at a critical time in my life, the belief I had that *they should know better* shifted. Because they simply didn't. Cognitively, this work helped me understand how I became who I am.

If you have reached this point in this book, perhaps you are becoming aware by now that the only person who can take responsibility for doing the inner work and making change is you. Each one of us comes from unique circumstances and dynamics in our family of origin. Sometimes blame and anger towards our parents is appropriate. But our power comes back to us when we take responsibility for our life and our healing. The past and other people cannot be changed. We can choose what we want to carry forward into our lives. What are *your* beliefs? How do *you* want to feel? What do *you* want and need? What do you need to embrace or let go of to have the life you truly desire? The answers are all inside, not outside, of you.

An Invitation to Excavate Your Family History

This invitation is about familiarizing yourself with your parents' or primary caregivers' history. Reflect on the questions below, noting any others that might come up for you, and take any actions that resonate. Use your journal to capture important insights.

- What was the relationship between your parents or primary caregivers like? How did they communicate with each other?

- What kind of home environment did your parents or primary caregivers grow up in? What was their relationship like with their parents?

- Research attachment theory to discover your pattern.* Notice any connections with your family history.

  Note that attachment patterns can exist on a spectrum, and can sometimes change in certain circumstances and with the right partner. For example, someone with an anxious or avoidant attachment pattern who partners up with someone with a secure attachment pattern can experience healing in that dynamic. For this exercise, search for the original pattern you developed.

- What connections can you make between your romantic history and your relationship with your parents or primary caregivers?

If you are having trouble making these connections, it is useful to know that not all questions will have a straightforward answer. And it's not necessary to have all the answers to work on your healing. Trust that the clues sit inside of you already. Even when we don't have vivid childhood memories with details we can easily recall, we can pick up on other information stored in our subconscious mind. You might benefit from asking yourself, "Is this pattern or behavior truly mine, or was it learned?"

The Takeaway

Looking at our childhood and family history helps us understand our context, what we have learned or inherited from our parents, their parents, and so on. It helps us see the beliefs and patterns we are born into, and how they influence us today through the lens of our choices. When we connect the dots between our present and the past, we can make the invisible visible and build a new relationship with what we learn. We become more empowered to take responsibility for who we really are and make aligned choices. The healing process of shifting beliefs or behaviors that no longer serve us creates space for the most authentic version of who we are to come forth. Our Brave Wise Woman dwells underneath our patterning and history.

NOTE: If you've experienced trauma or abuse in your childhood, I encourage you to work with a trauma specialist.

Lesson 6

Yes Is an Invitation to Let Go and Grow

"The big question is whether you are going to be able to say a hearty yes to your adventure."

- Joseph Campbell, *The Power of Myth*

What are you still holding onto that hurts your heart or prevents you from growing? What would be possible for your life if you could let that go?

I believe we know what we cling on to and why. Following loss, we can hold on to emotional states because they keep us connected. We can long for a life we no longer live. We can cling to ideas and perceptions about others, and even ourselves. We can hold on firmly to our comfort zone because change can feel scary.

What we cannot let go of, we are attached to. Attachment means we want situations, people, and even ourselves to be a certain way. We can attach to things like cars, shoes, and a job title as much as people, perspectives, and opinions because we assign meaning to them, usually a belief that they communicate who we are. Our attachments create resistance to growth. When we're on a healing path or going through change, eventually we realize they keep us stuck and prevent us from receiving what comes next. With the medicine of curiosity, we can ask, *Is holding onto this person, this situation, this feeling, this belief, this perception of myself still useful to me?*

This is a simple but big question. After all, we can hold onto anything, even if there's no obvious reason to do so anymore, and find a way to justify it.

But as I rebuilt my life, this question became a teacher on my journey of self-discovery. It helped me notice it was time to expand my comfort zone— the one driven by the belief that *certainty keeps me safe.*

Certainty and Uncertainty

Tony Robbins often speaks to the six human needs that drive our decisions. Two of them are certainty and uncertainty.

- Certainty is about assurance. Humans want to move towards pleasure and avoid pain. When we make decisions that support our need for certainty, we are seeking security and familiarity.

- Uncertainty is about variety. Humans are also wired to evolve and grow. Decisions that lead us outside our comfort zone support our need for newness or change.

I tend to make decisions based on certainty because I want to feel safe. It's a way to control my reality. But the only thing certain about the experience of divorce is that the marriage is over. Everything else is a state of uncertainty. And yet, I had attachments to that relationship. The decision to reclaim my maiden name was painful because my identity was tied to my married name. I was attached to it because of what I believed it communicated about me. Since I had an unconscious belief that *marriage was an accomplishment*, I had achieved what society communicated was desirable. So, the idea of being known as Maiden Name Me again brought up shame. I didn't think highly of that previous version of me; the young woman who made errors in judgment and was ignorant of her patterns and blind spots. It took multiple conversations with myself and others to realize I could change my self-perception. To do that, I had to stop resisting the flow of what was happening, stay open to insights, and accept that my life as I knew it was changing. I also had to practice expanding my comfort zone by saying yes and embracing the uncertainty that goes along with it to redefine myself.

#SayYes was Born

Early on in my heartbreak, social media became a creative outlet for me to express the swirl I was experiencing inside. While searching for a hashtag to include in a post one day, I wondered, *If I had a personal hashtag to mark this time in my life, what would it be?* #SayYes came to mind. It was a passing thought, mostly, but it became the genesis of what helped me edge outside of my comfort zone. Rather than use it on social media, it became an informal filter for everyday decisions that I might normally say no to. On a small scale, #SayYes helped me get out of the house and spend time with friends when I didn't feel like it. On a bigger note, #SayYes helped me meet different parts of myself and do things I never thought I would do. #SayYes became an invitation to let go and grow.

As I practiced applying it to my decision-making, I discovered a new relationship with *yes* and what it looks like for me.

The No–Yes

The No–Yes emerges after defining what is a no for me. In other words, by saying no to something, I create space for learning what is a yes for me.

After the split, my path became more about *tuning in* rather than *tuning out*. During this time,

I noticed how much I hated television. It was always on during my marriage. Because it represented *tuning out,* it was a clear no. The day I realized it had to go, I gave it back to my ex-husband. I was making space for more of whatever would become a yes.

Around that time, I dove into music to fill the empty space in my life and help me through. I began to explore different genres as well as global music. The more I listened, the more I noticed music engaged my mind, heart, and body. I liked how that felt.

I began to #SayYes to music all the time. From morning to night, music was on in the home. I'd clean the house with it on. I'd listen to it while working. It didn't take long to build up a music library of over thirteen hundred of my favorites. Music became a friend and companion. It lifted me out of loneliness or sadness and held me as I rode emotional waves. Music emerged as a clear yes in my life because I loved the way it felt in my soul.

The I'll–Try–It–Yes

Curiosity about trying something new drives the I'll–Try–It–Yes for me.

One day at lunch with my girlfriend she said, "Jen, I have an idea for you." She pulled out her phone and showed me her friend's social media account. In one of the photos, her friend was dressed in a bodysuit, standing on a hill, and gazing into the horizon. With her hands on her hips, and strands of wind-swept hair gently hugging her cheeks, she looked confident and free.

I grabbed the phone from her hand to inspect the image. It stirred something inside, and I realized I wanted to feel the way she looked.

"Wow!"

"She looks amazing, right? You should do it too!"

The idea appealed. By this time, I knew I was better off without my ex but was hesitant about the idea of dating again in midlife. I wanted to explore how an experience like this might boost my confidence.

I browsed the photographer's website when I got home. After an introductory consultation with him about my goals, I booked a session. I was nervous, but something inside me screamed #SayYes!

In the weeks leading up to the shoot, I collaborated with the photographer to plan my outfits. On the day of the shoot, I had my hair and makeup done and drove to meet him on location. Anticipating how the day would unfold was both terrifying and exciting. What made my heart pound out of my chest was expressing a side of myself I was still getting to know, then capturing it in a photograph. I wasn't sure how to pose, and it felt *so awkward*. Whatever I was doing felt fake to me— like I was *trying* rather than *being*. But he helped me find some ease by sharing tips on how to hold my gaze and feel into the experience. My eyes lit up with excitement when he showed me a few test shots. They gave me the confidence to relax even more. I drove home that day smiling, feeling positive and upbeat.

The next morning, I woke up to a text message from him with a handful of images he had processed overnight.

They exceeded my expectations, and I noticed my response to each one was, *That is not me!*

The last image he sent that morning moved me to tears. I was standing in a field, my head tilted up towards the sun with my eyes closed. My hair cascaded down my back with my long gold earrings entwined in its waves.

Who is that woman?

I didn't recognize myself.

I didn't see Maiden Name Me, and it wasn't Married Name Me in the photo. It was a version of me I hadn't met yet: a strong woman on the verge of stepping into her power. An inexplicable shift had already occurred inside of me from the photoshoot experience, but it wasn't until I saw the photos that morning that I knew what it was.

It was time to reframe the question, *Am I good enough for my partners?* to: *Are they good enough for me?*

The Yes–Yes

The Yes–Yes emerges from a place of confidence, clarity, and calm within me. What experiences have you longed for? What do you want to do that aligns with your truth? My big answer was that it was time to work with plant medicine. For seven years, I had been curious about the path of healing and wisdom that comes from working with ayahuasca. I learned a lot about its healing potential by talking to people who have worked with this medicine.

My decision did not come lightly. Ayahuasca is a psychoactive tea that originates in South America, made from the *Banisteriopsis Caapi* and *Psychotria Viridis* plants.[2] Amazonian tribes have used it as a ceremonial, spiritual medicine. Through altered states of consciousness, the places in our life that need healing or wisdom can be explored. The experience can be illuminating, but it can also be unpredictable and unlock what you didn't know needed to be unlocked within. If you are truly called to work with this medicine, they say you will feel it in your heart when the time is right. The finality of my divorce was that moment.

When you #SayYes to this work and commit, it's more than attending a ceremony. The period leading up to it is a time of contemplation and preparation in

---

2   Additional research and education is recommended for those who are curious about this plant medicine. Understand and abide by the laws in your country regarding ayahuasca and consult a medical doctor.

the mind and the body. Not only do you cleanse your body by eliminating certain medicines and specific types of food from your diet, but you disengage from external distractions: television, phone, and social media. Even those experiences show us what we need to see.

I was a good student of the preparation process and followed all the instructions. I also went down the rabbit hole of researching the internet to learn more about ceremony preparation and got a taste of the volume of conflicting information. *The instructions are to eat a vegetarian diet. But this internet source says, no bananas, tomatoes, or spinach. Can I eat those foods or not?* Each new piece of information I found led to more questions and confusion. I became stricter and more diligent about what I ate, worried about what would happen to me if I wasn't. The stress manifested as a back spasm.

The ceremony opened with a brief talk and a blessing of the medicine. One by one, we took turns approaching the altar to receive our cup of tea, pausing before consuming it to offer an intention. My intention was to be shown what I needed to learn about self-doubt so I could step more fully into my power. The tea was thick, bitter, and earthy—not tasty or smooth at all—but not as awful as I had imagined.

Within forty-five minutes, I felt the medicine take effect in my body. Heat rushed up through my back to my head and then a beautiful cosmic universe made up of sacred geometry and twisting, pulsing shapes was visible. I became fidgety, and with my back spasm, it was hard to get comfortable, but I eventually settled into a half-sitting, half lying-down position. As the *icaros*—traditional indigenous Amazonian healing songs—continued, I fixated on the visuals: the awe of the cosmic universe had opened up to me.

Through the wisdom of this plant medicine, I could see that my patterns leading up to the ceremony were what I needed to examine: the questions and concerns and getting bogged down in the details to create a false sense of certainty and control. This was the work for me to do, and that clarity informed the path I was already on. The inherent questions for me to contemplate and integrate were, *Where does security come from? Are we ever really certain?* I'm still working on chipping away at this today.

What I now understand about my Yes–Yes decisions is that they come from my inner knowing and a desire to claim the experiences I want in my life, without hesitation, worry, or fear. They speak through my Brave Wise Woman.

An Invitation to #SayYes

- What will you #SayYes to today? Find an opportunity to expand your comfort zone and reflect on what you learned.

If you feel called to do so, I invite you to share a photo of your #SayYes experience on Instagram and tag me: @jenlegaspi.coach

The Takeaway

The word *yes* can be a medicine just as much as the word *no*. It depends on our context and patterns. For those who have people-pleasing behavior, learning to say no and set boundaries is the path to growth and self-love.

For those who prefer lots of certainty and resist change, the practice is saying yes and staying open to what emerges. When we say yes to our expansion, we create opportunities to shift our self-perceptions and beliefs about who we are. Our experiences invite us to let go of whatever isn't serving our life. Our bravery is also called forward, which changes our relationship to the fear of uncertainty.

While we might step outside our comfort zone to be adventurous, we might not choose to do that thing we did again. But a Yes–Yes decision is a *fuck yes*; a claiming of what we want for our life. Not only can we experience more personal fulfillment, but we discover the courage to be the women *we already are* but hadn't known yet until we made that choice.

Questioning and releasing our attachments is ultimately a journey of acceptance, change, and growth. The Brave Wise Woman walks this path.

Want more?

Amplify your healing journey with this companion to the lessons in this book:

8 Powerful Intentions for Awakening Your Brave Wise Woman

Visit www.bravewisewoman.com to receive your gift and join a community of women who will receive exclusive tips and offers for upcoming programs to help you meet your Brave Wise Woman.

Lesson 7

Closure is a Conversation with Self

"With time, patience and work you can reach a better place:
A place of healing, happiness and closure."

- **Michael Louis Eads, A Man's Feelings**

When a significant relationship ends, it's natural to want closure. It's part of the healing process. But not every ending wraps up in a perfect bow. Not every partner wants to *consciously uncouple*. Endings can be messy and complicated.

I had claimed truth as one of my values in marriage but realized I had difficulty embodying it in that relationship. I also didn't understand my ex-husband's truth. What happened between us that led to the end? In the beginning, I spent a lot of energy wanting clarity, which I hoped would come from him.

I believed that our separation would create the space for us to have a deeper conversation. But we can't force someone else's readiness and my belief led to disappointment. Though I was frustrated and desperate for answers, my intuition told me I might never fully know his truth. If I wanted answers, I had to seek them out on my own. I had to find my truth. In the months that followed, I continued to analyze our relationship. As I did so, I pinpointed dynamics that I believe contributed to our downfall.

When we expand our interests, we naturally grow and evolve. As I became more interested in personal development—attending workshops, the evolution of my yoga practice, getting additional education and certifications, and exploring healing through different modalities—my spiritual side emerged. I was headed in a new direction. He was on a different path. I didn't realize it then, but I was already in the process of peeling back the layers to meet my Brave Wise Woman, and I believe it was a contributing reason we grew apart. I understand now that the energy of doing inner work has potential to erode the foundation of relationships built on inauthenticity.

As I changed, I took on his personal challenges as if they were my own. I lectured him in an effort to help him change and grow too. Looking back, I realized my intentions may not have been as pure as they seemed. On an unconscious level, my sense of security was threatened and to protect it, I ended up trying to control him in an attempt to get my needs met. What I know now that I didn't know then is that our partner's challenges are *their* responsibility to address when *they are ready*. We cannot force others to change. And if we place our sense of security in the hands of others, we are giving away our power.

Once I dove deeper into my healing, I realized that my childhood experiences influenced how I showed up in our relationship. What I learned (or didn't learn) from my parents about communication was obvious. My fear of speaking up and fear of abandonment were red flags in our relationship, and I made assumptions from a wounded place within me about marriage. Relationships are living entities and ours wasn't nurtured over time. Instead, little moments of dissatisfaction stacked up and became enormous walls. I believe the relationship died a slow death, and I didn't see it coming.

But the hardest part for me to come to terms with, especially at the beginning, was the truth that our commitment wasn't as solid as I thought it was. I entered into marriage believing it was forever. As I took baby steps to rebuild my life and make some emotional headway, sometimes two steps backward were unavoidable, such as when I received the screenshot that hinted at the possibility of someone new in his life. I retreated into a dark hole of sadness and had to figure out how to climb out and into balance. A part of me wanted to show him how much I was hurting, but I didn't. My initial reason was because it was tough enough to be in the middle of divorce negotiations without layering on another difficult conversation.

"I'll do it after we're done negotiating," I told my friends.

I was navigating more than the divorce process; I was navigating complex emotions, including moments of humiliation and despair. Despite that, a part of me knew I would not let this time in my life define me. I often envisioned myself emerging victoriously from the ashes.

As the divorce negotiations progressed, my friends pressed on, "Are you planning to talk to him now?"

I continued to hit the pause button. Yes, the divorce process had progressed but so had my healing. Every day, I imagined myself trying to talk to him and asked myself, *What do I hope to gain from this conversation?* Then I waited for an answer to emerge.

As I continued with this daily inquiry and patiently waited for an answer, I noticed it was helping me trust my inner wisdom for the first time in my life. It felt good to be patient, and it helped me develop my patience muscle. But a part of me must have been conflicted. One night, I dreamt he was moving out of state. In the dream, I felt a deep urge to confront him. But sitting with that inquiry over and over and patiently waiting for an answer taught me that sometimes our power doesn't come from confrontation but in turning inward and trusting. What I knew by then was that he had someone else. I also realized I lacked the awareness and inner tools to show up as the partner I thought I could be because I wasn't showing up for myself first. As my self-exploration continued, my inquiry shifted:

What did I expect to hear him say or learn from him that I didn't already know deep inside? Do I need external validation of my truth for it to be true?

Though I contemplated these questions over and over, I never received an answer that felt like a confrontation would honor where I was at in my life. Instead, the steps I took each day—whether forward or backward, then forward again—while grieving and consciously calling forward the medicines within me to help me through was my path to closure. In each moment, I was learning who I was, how to care for my heart, about self-acceptance and taking responsibility for my life. I was learning to trust the process. Healing was happening in my own time and in the way I intuitively navigated it. As I connected the dots in my life, I eventually reached a point of not caring about his why. One day, it simply didn't matter to me. Confronting him about it was not an action aligned with the me I was becoming. I had the answers and knew my truth. The more time passed, the more I trusted it.

That experience taught me a big lesson on my journey. The truth within us is a powerful medicine. When we connect with it and trust it, our behaviors and actions can align with the wisest, most authentic version of self.

***

Two years later, it was time to sell property we still owned. As we were discussing logistics, he mentioned he was planning to move away. My heart fell into my stomach when I realized this was the dream I'd had two years prior!

Emotionally, I wasn't in the same spot as I was in the dream. My life had also settled into a new rhythm. Acceptance had set in; I had my answers. My healing journey had progressed and I felt complete.

Still, I said, "I'd like for us to meet up and talk." To my surprise, he agreed.

We met at a local restaurant after work. We ordered a round of drinks and exchanged small talk, updating each other on our jobs, his pending move, and our plans for selling our property.

"I've been doing the work to understand my responsibility for what happened in our marriage," I said. "I know my path was part of what contributed to us growing apart. And, your personal challenges were never mine to take on, but I did. I pushed you when I shouldn't have. I'm sorry for that. But no matter what I did, I did not deserve to have our marriage end the way it did."

I paused. He sat quietly and listened.

"I've known about the woman in your life for a while. And I want you to know, I wish you luck with your new life."

My words were succinct, my voice calm. My Brave Wise Woman had emerged. She didn't need to cry, waver, or doubt herself. She didn't get into any details. She was confident and clear and revealed herself through curiosity, patience, faith, courage, and trusting the process as much as she trusted herself to navigate the journey. As soon as I spoke up, I felt sparkly and free.

"I'm sorry," he said.

His words didn't faze me. I didn't meet him that day to receive an apology or to confront him. I met up to take responsibility for my role in the demise of our marriage and clear that energy from my system. I had reached a quiet place of self-forgiveness—not for him or what happened—but for the assumptions I made about who I was, about our marriage, and about what I couldn't or didn't want to see both in him and myself. I had forgiven myself *for not knowing*.

Even if this conversation with him had never happened, I knew I was complete. I had what I needed. All of us are always whole and complete, even in our most trying times. When we seek our answers within and trust our truth, we prove to ourselves that we are.

An Invitation to Reflect on Closure

Reflect on the following questions as journal prompts:

- What does closure look like to you? How will you know when you have it? How will you feel?
- What truths do you already have inside of you?
- Where in your body do you connect to your truth? Can you describe what it feels like?

Closure is an acceptance and letting go process that takes time and can look different for each of us. It calls for the medicines of patience and courage to navigate the difficult moments. The more we bravely question our attachments and focus our attention on what we can take responsibility for, the more we can know our truth and find our power. The closure process is fluid, ebbing and flowing with our healing path until the intensity of the difficulty subsides, and we have clarity in mind, body, and spirit.

Closure differs from forgiveness. Closure is about coming to terms with a situation, while forgiveness is about releasing. What they share is a slow-burn process of acceptance and letting go with the result of inner peace and freedom. When the time is right to consider the possibility of forgiveness, anger or resentment, and other emotions, won't have as strong of an energetic charge inside of you. You might contemplate: *What do I need next for my inner peace?*

The Takeaway

Closure is being at peace with the outcome—even if you wanted a different ending or you felt wronged. Even if it takes years to arrive in that place. We always have a choice about how we want to experience life. Each moment, we can choose how we want our path to unfold. If we wait for or rely on others to provide us with closure, not only might we never receive it, but we are also giving our power away by holding our life back to wait for someone else. The work after a significant breakup is to grieve and to allow that process to take place. As painful as it can feel sometimes, we are the only ones who can do this for ourselves. When we accept closure as an empowering conversation with ourselves and go through the grief journey, our truth will reveal itself with the medicines of patience, nurturance, and self-compassion. Once known, it can never be invalidated by another. Our truth is our power, our inner peace, and our connection to our Brave Wise Woman.

When we commit to our healing, we eventually come to see that our mental and emotional energy belongs *to us for us* to harness in ways that serve our highest good, instead of being at the mercy of our stories. The stories we tell ourselves hijack our progress and freedom. At some point, we realize we have the power to release the energy of situations that are taking up this precious mental and emotional energy. This is where forgiveness comes in.

Forgiveness is a journey we take *for us*, not for the other person or to condone what has happened, and it usually becomes a choice after feeling all the emotions about the situation and processing them. Forgiveness is saying *I love myself and I don't want to carry this negative energy around*. It's another self-love practice. The best part is, like closure, it doesn't have to be a conversation with anyone but yourself.

Want more?

Amplify your healing journey with this companion to the lessons in this book:

8 Powerful Intentions for Awakening Your Brave Wise Woman

Visit www.bravewisewoman.com to receive your gift and join a community of women who will receive exclusive tips and offers for upcoming programs to help you meet your Brave Wise Woman.

Lesson 8

Self-Love is a Practice of Coming Back to Our Truth

"How you love yourself is how you teach others to love you."

– Rupi Kaur

After jumping from one relationship to another for *at least* twenty years, I took a three-and-a-half year break from a serious relationship to get to know myself. I now understood my romantic patterns and choices and the impact my childhood and my parents' history had on me. Taking responsibility for peeling back these layers of the onion had gifted me with options for what happens next in my life. I had more tools and practices. I continued with my version of meditation, practiced responding rather than reacting to situations, and continued to trust the Universe by saying yes to new experiences. Maiden Name Me 2.0 had blossomed.

When I met my next romantic partner, a new layer of healing became possible. With the new awareness of my wounds, patterns, and context, I practiced making self-honoring choices. In doing so, I taught myself how to show up as a woman who loves herself.

I could sense this new man wasn't like the other men I had dated. He was confident, down-to-earth, and easy to talk to.

Because of the insights I had learned on my journey, it was clear I needed to ask my dates early on about their relationship with their parents.

"I know it's premature to bring this up, but I'm curious about your relationship with your father."

"My dad's awesome. We get along great."

"So you're close?"

"Yes."

I was relieved to hear that I had finally met someone who did not have a difficult relationship with his father.

What else did my healing journey teach me? I learned that healing does not mean that our wounds completely disappear. But as we become more conscious of their presence, and the patterns we've developed because of them, we can navigate our life differently and shift the relationship with our wounds, ourselves, and others too.

How did I show up in this relationship? What changed?

***

Clarity and Personal Boundaries

An outcome of my inner work up to that point was greater clarity about who I was and what I wanted out of my next serious relationship: a co-creation of experiences for mutual growth. I was not looking to just *have someone* or for another person to fill a perceived void within me.

Openly discussing my vision of a relationship set the tone for how I wanted to show up as a partner. I knew I had to walk the talk and had the tools and knowledge to support me to do that. It was time to bravely practice using them.

I also had clarity about staying in my lane. What does this mean? I set a personal boundary for what is mine vs. his to take responsibility for. I take responsibility for my triggers, wounds, life direction, and commitment to growth and healing. In action, this looks like avoiding blame, looking within for my answers, communicating my needs, and practicing new tools and skills. My partner is responsible for his triggers, personal challenges and direction of his life.

Meeting My Attachment Needs

Now that I understand my attachment pattern, I have a greater awareness of how to work with it in a relationship. Noticing when anxiety is present, identifying my needs, and meeting them is the practice. The more I can do this, the more I can bring conscious awareness into my relationship rather than unconsciously projecting my stuff onto my partner.

One way that I work with my attachment needs is by paying attention to the stories that I tell myself about my partner or our relationship. In Byron Katie's book *Loving What Is*, she writes, "The truth is prior to every story. Every story, prior to investigation, prevents us from seeing what's true." I use a simplified inquiry based on "The Work," which is fully detailed in her book. I ask myself, *What's true at this moment?* By examining what is true, I create space between reaction and response to avoid jumping to conclusions and projecting my need for reassurance onto my partner.

Here's an example of what my mental process looks like:

What's true is… I notice he is being quieter than normal right now.

What's true is… My heart is beating faster than normal. My mind is racing. I am feeling anxiety.

What's true is... There are many reasons he might be quiet. It does not automatically mean something is wrong with our relationship. I have no proof that it does.

What's true is... I have a need for connection at this moment. How can I meet my needs?

My partner and I shared the understanding that triggers are not about the other person but the pain within us. So, when I'm triggered, investigating the source and uncovering my needs is my work. As I practice, I've learned that inquiry and the medicine of trust are helpful allies on the healing path. The more I examine what is really true and trust it, the more self-reliant and secure within I become. Questioning my thoughts is a practice of self-love.

Reparenting My Inner Child

No matter what age we are today, we are also the past. It is believed our past is housed in the subconscious mind, where we can find our inner child. Our inner child is the young part of us that is sensitive and vulnerable. She expresses curiosity, joy, and creativity and invites us to be playful, to laugh, and feel free. But she is also the part of us that has unmet needs from childhood and is connected to our attachment patterns. Her presence is noticeable when we become triggered and reactive, or when we are overwhelmed or stressed out. How does your inner child show up in these circumstances?

Inner child work is about developing a relationship with this young part, making it safe for her to speak to you through her language of feelings, and uncovering her unmet needs. It helps us see how our present-day reactions are linked to our past. Reparenting her is about meeting her needs and giving her what she didn't receive so she can feel seen, heard, acknowledged, and safe. It helps us more fully embrace our wholeness and heal the wounded part of us that continues to show up in our adult lives.

The first time I did inner child work to meet Little Jen, I learned she loved to play but was tentative about trying new things. She was afraid of making mistakes and getting in trouble with her parents. It was more comforting for Little Jen to stay hidden; she loved to play in her closet because it made her feel safe. This initial work gave me insight into the origins of my perfectionist tendencies.

When I'm stressed or anxious, I know my inner child is speaking to me. One of the ways I've practiced reparenting her in real time is by placing one hand on my belly, one on my heart, closing my eyes, and exhaling deeply to calm my nerves. I visualize my heart space as a gateway to Little Jen. I breathe into that space. I then ask her what she's feeling and what she needs, and listen for the answers. Then I silently reassure her, *It's going to be OK. I've got this. You are safe. Don't worry. I love you.* I repeat it over and over again until I feel softening within me.

The relationship to our inner child can take time to develop. She can be shy or not trusting of us at first and our ability to nurture her can sometimes feel elusive. The work is to practice forging a connection anyway, so she can open up, we can hear the words she's been eager to speak, and our adult self can give her the unconditional love she craves. When the relationship solidifies, it supports us to heal, to access our authenticity, and to love who we are.

Meeting Challenging Moments with Truth

No relationship is without challenges, and those moments are our teachers. How do we choose to show up for them? How do we respond?

Challenging moments become more challenging when one or both people don't have tools to communicate in a healthy way. This was my experience in the past. But as I learned to trust my healing path, I grew more confident. That confidence has become the fuel for how I show up and practice breaking my old communication pattern. I practice meeting my fear with truth and wisdom.

In a deep conversation with my partner one night, I chose to speak my truth.

"There are no guarantees in a relationship. Even with marriage, there are no guarantees of a future together. We grow and evolve over time, and that calls for acceptance and patience. Hopefully, the other grows and evolves in alignment. But there are no guarantees that will happen. So, the question becomes, what kind of experience do you want to have? Choose that. And, if this relationship is a true no for you, let's not waste any more time."

He let my words sink in, then looked me in the eye and said, "Wow. You are fully in your power right now. Go on, I'm listening."

The Brave Wise Woman within me had found her voice in a relationship. I recognize her because she is the part of me that speaks with clarity, presence, and evenness. She is unafraid to speak her truth and does not fear the response. She knows she can handle what comes next because the outcome is aligned with her truth. I've learned the more I can call her forward and speak through her instead of through the pain of my inner child, the more my partner can hear and receive my message.

An Invitation to Meet Your Younger Self

Ready to meet your inner child? Before you do this exercise, it's helpful to remember:

- Anyone can have unmet childhood needs, even those from happy homes.

- You do not have to have specific memories of your childhood to do this work. If the details seem fuzzy, focus on the feelings or the energy, and trust the information in your subconscious mind.

- Some who have a deeply wounded inner child from situations such as abuse or neglect, for example, may find it beneficial to do this work with the help of a licensed professional.

Instructions:

Find a photo of yourself as a child, perhaps at an age you know you had an unmet need. If nothing comes to mind, any photo from your childhood will do.

1. Gaze at this photo for a couple minutes.

2. What do you notice about your younger self? Do you see happiness? Sadness? Joy?

3. Greet your inner child with a warm hello.

4. Ask her: *Do you have any messages for me today?* Listen.

5. Ask her: *What are you feeling right now?* Listen.

6. Ask her: *What do you need from me today?* Listen.

7. Based on what she says, what words could you say to the younger version of you that would feel nurturing for her to hear? How can you meet her needs? Speak directly to her either out loud or quietly inside.

8. If she is shy or doesn't speak to you today, tell her: *It's OK. Thank you so much. I love you. I'll connect with you again soon.*

Spend a little time in reflection afterward and journal whatever comes up for you.

Keep this photo visible to remind yourself of your inner child's constant presence. A photo of myself, age three, sits at my desk. The innocence, vulnerability, and joy on her face remind me that part of me is still alive.

The Takeaway

We don't have to have all our childhood wounds healed to be in a relationship. But as teachers and mirrors, relationships will always show us who we are, the progress of our growth and evolution, and where we have more healing work to do. When the Brave Wise Woman finds her voice in a relationship, she inspires healthier relationship dynamics because she is grounded in her truth.

In her book *Recovery of Your Inner Child*, Lucia Capacchione, Ph.D., writes, "Experts have estimated that ninety-five percent of the population received inadequate parenting." We all have an inner child who needs some attention, even those who had a happy childhood. When we are triggered and reactive, imagine your inner child has a set of keys to your car and she is driving. *Is allowing her to drive useful for your life?* By developing a closer bond with her and helping her feel seen, heard, and safe, our capacity to respond rather than react grows. It forges a deeper relationship with ourselves, including more attunement to our triggers, emotions, and needs. Nobody else but us can acknowledge and care for that young, tender part of ourselves. Being the kind of parent to her we wish we had is a practice of self-love. Give yourself the love you deserve.

When we walk a healing path, we do it to have a healthier relationship with ourselves first, to know the different layers of ourselves more intimately. Our roots grow deeper and support us in practicing coming back to our truth, to our Brave Wise Woman.

Final Thoughts on Healing and Self-Love

it did not
happen overnight
and it was not
given to me by another

i am the maker
of the happiness and love
growing within me

- yung pueblo, inward

Before my journey, if I had been asked to explain self-love, I would not have been able to. I had not yet done the deeper inner work to see how I was abandoning myself to receive the love I craved. Once I became conscious of my wounds and patterns, I transformed my breakup into my power by confidently practicing making self-honoring choices, and through them, embodying more self-love.

What have I learned about healing and self-love?

I've discovered healing *is a journey without a final destination.* It's an ongoing practice of curiosity, courage, acceptance, and letting go. The process invites us to greet all of our layers with compassion. When the beliefs, patterns and behaviors that no longer serve our deepest desires are revealed, we are called to transform them. As we do, we meet more of our authentic self. It is there that we receive the gift and honor of knowing our Brave Wise Woman.

Through our Brave Wise Woman, we know we are not at the mercy of our stories. We are empowered to make aligned *choices* for our lives; ones reflected in our words, behaviors, actions and outcomes. When we embody her presence, we show others what clarity, inner peace, and truth in action look like, and in that place, rightfully claim our voice and power.

As we embrace our wholeness, we realize we never lack. What we're seeking to fill the perception of a void is the medicine that already exists inside of us. Our source of internal truth is where the Brave Wise Woman lives. As our healing journey continues, embodying her presence and power in all areas of life becomes a self-love practice.

Brave Wise Women

Take responsibility for their healing

Know themselves deeply

Trust the process

Look within for their answers

Shift unhelpful beliefs and patterns

Learn from their choices

Honor themselves

Speak their truth

Forgive

Practice bravery every day

Sister, I wish you a beautiful process of exploration and self-discovery as you heal from your breakup. I hope your path leads you to meaningful insights, healing practices, and personal experience of self-love. Your Brave Wise Woman awaits you on the other side of your defining moment in life.

Love This Book? Help Others Discover It

Sister, thank you for reading this book.

I invite you to please leave me a book review! Every review matters, and I'd love to hear from you.

Head over to Amazon or wherever you purchased this book to leave an honest review for me.

Acknowledgments

Writing this book with the desire to serve and inspire other women was a difficult, vulnerable, and transformative journey. I gained more from the process than I could have ever imagined. But this path was not walked alone and not without many soul supporters in my life.

I'm eternally grateful to Kerk Murray, my book coach at Self-Publishing School. From our first conversation, he believed in the power of my story and helped me to believe in myself. And to my editor, Sandra Wissinger, whose sisterhood and wisdom helped my book come to fruition.

I'm eternally grateful to my family of origin. Mom, thank you for giving me your shoulder to cry on during my heartbreaks, for seeing me as the woman I have become, and for your ongoing encouragement. Dad, your wounds lit the path. It took a long time, but I see you now for who you are and who you've always been. Dom, thank you for showing up for me during my darkest moments. I love you all.

Enakshi, Stefanie, and Liz, I'm deeply grateful for your support as amazing women, friends, and sounding boards on this book journey.

Thank you, Eddie, for your unwavering support and trust in the process while I wrote.

Bradford, Carl, Gita, Jacqui, Maxine, Thad, and Toma, your support at a delicate time helped me to heal and fly. Thank you from the bottom of my heart.

Sand, you've been an amazing mentor. Your divine wisdom at the eleventh hour was gold. Thank you for your support, the transmission of spiritual teachings, and your medicine of graciousness.

Scott, it's an honor to have worked with you. Your mastery behind the camera is magic.

To all the unseen teachers on my path: Fear, Love, Doubt, Courage, Curiosity, Patience, Beginnings, Endings, Truth, and Change. I'm grateful to be your student in this lifetime.

And to my readers, who have taken one step closer to meeting the Brave Wise Woman living inside of them. You inspire me.

Finally, with deepest respect and gratitude, gracias Madre.

How to Connect and Work with Jen

All photography by Scott David Burgess © 2022

As a coach, Jen's greatest joy is empowering women to reclaim their truth, forge a more loving relationship with themselves, and live an authentic, brave life so our communities can thrive.

She is a certified coach with Elementum Coaching Institute and a certified yoga teacher. She also has an integrative life coaching certificate and, like a good girl, has earned her M.B.A.

Learn more: jenlegaspi.com

When you sign up for her email list at www.bravewisewoman.com, you'll receive *8 Powerful Intentions to Awaken Your Brave Wise Woman* as a gift. You'll also join a community of women who will receive exclusive tips and offers for upcoming programs to help you meet your Brave Wise Woman.

Follow her on Instagram: @jenlegaspi.coach

Email her at: jen@jenlegaspi.com

Influential Resources from my Journey

These resources were helpful to me on this leg of my healing journey; several were mentioned in this book. Many of these are still my go-to references. My development and growth continue to be influenced by them.

Mentioned in the book:

Attached, Amir Levine, M.D., and Rachel S.F. Heller, M.A,

   [2012], TarcherPerigee, page 12, 44-45

Bodily Maps of Emotions, Lauri Nummenmaa, Enrico Glerean, Riitta Hari and Jari K. Hietanen,

   [2013], Proceedings of the National Academy of Sciences (PNAS),

   https://www.pnas.org/doi/full/10.1073/pnas.1321664111

Breaking the Habit of Being Yourself, Dr. Joe Dispenza,

   [2013], Hay House Inc.

It Didn't Start with You, Mark Wolynn,

   [2010], Penguin Publishing Group, page 68

Loving What Is, Byron Katie,
  [2002], Harmony, page 86

Power vs. Force, David R. Hawkins M.D. Ph.D,
  [2014], Hay House Inc.

Recovery of Your Inner Child, Lucia Capacchione, Ph.D.,
  [1991], Touchstone, page 22

Other useful resources:

Adult Children of Emotionally Immature Parents, Lindsay C. Gibson, PsyD,
  [2015], New Harbinger Publications

Ayahuasca: Soul Medicine of the Amazon Jungle, Javier Regueiro,
  [2017], Lifestyle Entrepreneurs Press; 2nd edition

inward, yung pueblo,
  [2018], Andrews McMeel Publishing

The Untethered Soul, Michael A. Singer,
  [2007], New Harbinger Publications

Meditation: Blessings of Love, (11:26) Tara Brach,
 Guided Meditations

"A wise woman wishes to be no one's enemy; a wise woman refuses to be anyone's victim."

-Maya Angelou